Excel 2016 Guide

The basics
All you need to know about Excel

Dan N.

Copyright©2018 Dan N.
All Rights Reserved

Copyright © 2018 by Dan N.

All rights reserved. No part of this publication may be reproduced, distributed, or transmitted in any form or by any means, including photocopying, recording, or other electronic or mechanical methods, without the prior written permission of the author, except in the case of brief quotations embodied in critical reviews and certain other noncommercial uses permitted by copyright law.

Table of Contents

Introduction	5
Chapter 1- What is Excel?	6
Chapter 2- Excel Worksheets	8
Chapter 3- Formatting Cells	23
Chapter 4- Arithmetic Operations	37
Chapter 5- Validating, Grouping and Filters	41
Chapter 6- Data Sorting	56
Chapter 7- Ranges	58
Chapter 8- Formulas	60
Chapter 9- Working with Graphics	81
Chapter 10- Excel Macros	84
Chapter 11- Charts and Tables	90
Conclusion	99

Disclaimer

While all attempts have been made to verify the information provided in this book, the author does assume any responsibility for errors, omissions, or contrary interpretations of the subject matter contained within. The information provided in this book is for educational and entertainment purposes only. The reader is responsible for his or her own actions and the author does not accept any responsibilities for any liabilities or damages, real or perceived, resulting from the use of this information.

The trademarks that are used are without any consent, and the publication of the trademark is without permission or backing by the trademark owner. All trademarks and brands within this book are for clarifying purposes only and are the owned by the owners themselves, not affiliated with this document.

Introduction

Every organization generates and stores data. This data may become too large for processing and analysis by human beings. Human beings also understand visual representations more than numeric or textual data. Organizations need an easy way of analyzing data to get meaningful insights about the data. With Excel, this can be achieved. It comes with various tools that organizations can use to for data analysis. With Excel, organizations and individuals can get a visual way of representing their data. This can easily be achieved with Microsoft Excel. Excel comes with a feature known as "Macros". Macros provide Excel users with a way of automating tasks that they perform on a daily basis. It is also easy for to create Excel macros as they only have to record the tasks that they do, and the Macro will ensure that these are done correctly and sequentially every time. This book helps you understand the various features provided by Microsoft Excel and how to use them. Enjoy reading!

Chapter 1- What is Excel?

Excel, popularly referred to as *Microsoft Excel* is a product from Microsoft and the leading spreadsheet in the world. It provides a cell-by-cell layout which is a familiar and accessible way of displaying data. It also provides its users with an easy of drawing graphs and using calculation equations. For years, businesses have used Excel as the basis for building databases and for doing statistical analysis. Excel is also updated on a regular basis making it stay at the top. Note that Excel can run on Windows, Mac OS, Android and iOS, but not Windows alone as you might think. Excel is a powerful tool such that it even comes with its own programming language known as *Visual Basic for Applications (VBA)*. With VBA, one can develop software applications capable of accessing data stored in an Excel worksheet. These can provide users with an easy way of using Excel data, since one can come up with an application with an easy-to-use user interface that is integrated to Excel data. One can use a feature known as Macros to automate tasks that they do frequently in Excel. You only have to record the tasks as you do them and the macro will be created. After that, the macro will ensure that the tasks are done correctly and sequentially.

The excel sheets are made up of cells arranged in rows and columns. The rows are numbered while the columns have letter heads. Excel allows you to output your data in the form of line graphs, histograms and charts. With Excel, it is possible for you to create your own applications using a very simple programming language, that is, Visual Basic for Applications. To use Excel, you only have to install Microsoft Office as it comes bundled amongst the various Microsoft Office applications.

Chapter 2- Excel Worksheets

After starting Excel, a worksheet is normally created for you. A worksheet forms a very basic feature in Excel. Let us discuss the various operations involving worksheets in Excel:

Creating a New Worksheet

You may be working on a particular sheet and you need to start a new worksheet. This is because you may need to load some new data which is not related to the data in the current worksheet. This calls for you to create a new worksheet on which you can load the data. This can be done by following the steps given below:

1. Right click the name of the sheet then choose "Insert".

2. The Insert dialog will be presented. Choose "Worksheet" then click "Ok".

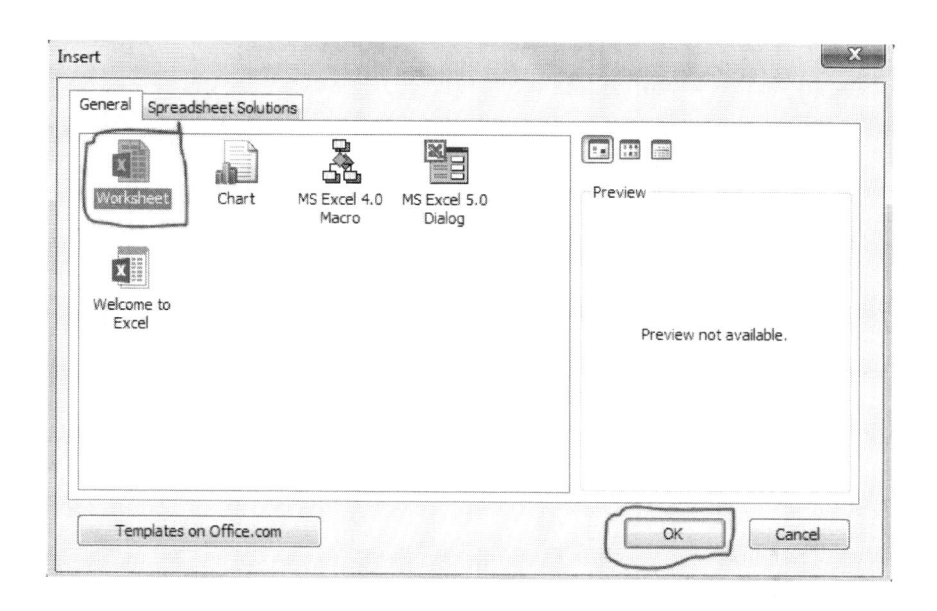

You will be presented with a new sheet on which you can begin to type your text.

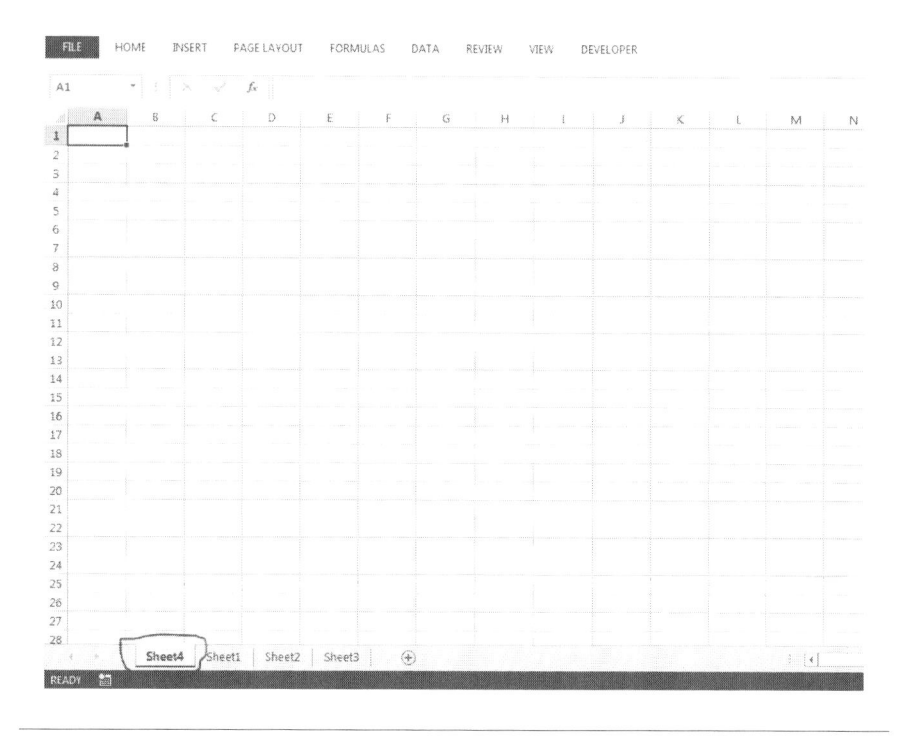

You can also use a keyboard shortcut to create a new worksheet. You can try pressing *Shift+F11* and you will get it. Once a sheet has been created, it is opened immediately so that you can begin using it.

Copying a Worksheet

Suppose we have the worksheet given below:

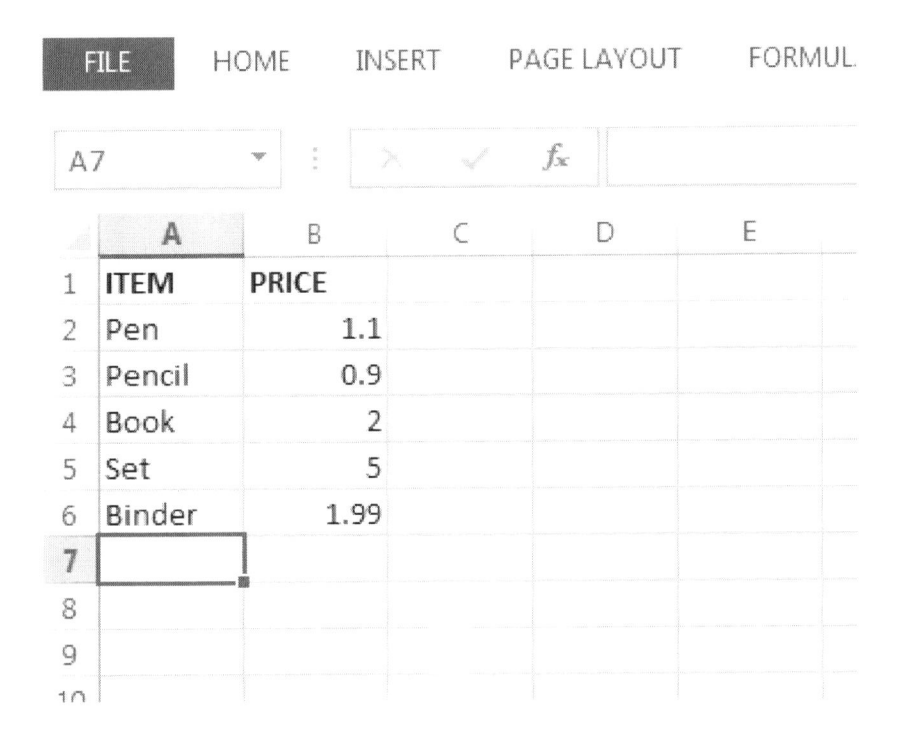

	A	B
1	ITEM	PRICE
2	Pen	1.1
3	Pencil	0.9
4	Book	2
5	Set	5
6	Binder	1.99

The following steps will help you copy the worksheet:

1. Right click the name of the sheet then choose "Move or Copy" option.

	A	B	C	D	E	F
1	ITEM	PRICE				
2	Pen	1.1				
3	Pencil	0.9				
4	Book	2				
5	Set	5				
6	Binder	1.99				
7						

Sheet4 | Sheet1 | Sheet2 | Sheet3

2. The Move or Copy dialog will be shown with the select Worksheet option you had chosen from the tab. Just click "Ok". Select the checkbox for "Create a copy" in order to create a copy of the

current sheet, then select the "move to end" option in order to create the copy at the end.

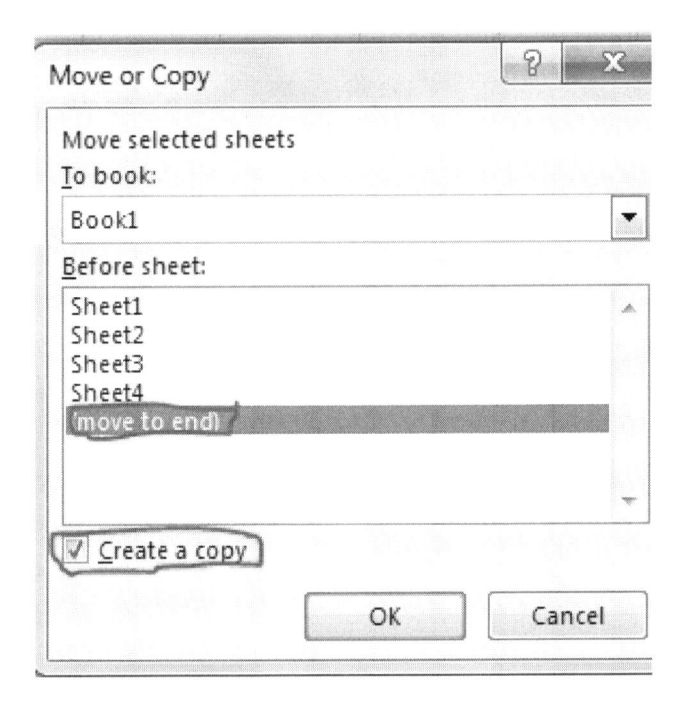

Click the "OK" button.

A new copy of the sheet should be created at the end. If you need to rename the sheet, just double click it and it will become editable. Enter a name like "Sheet5" the hit the enter key to save the changes. The new sheet will be given the name you have specified.

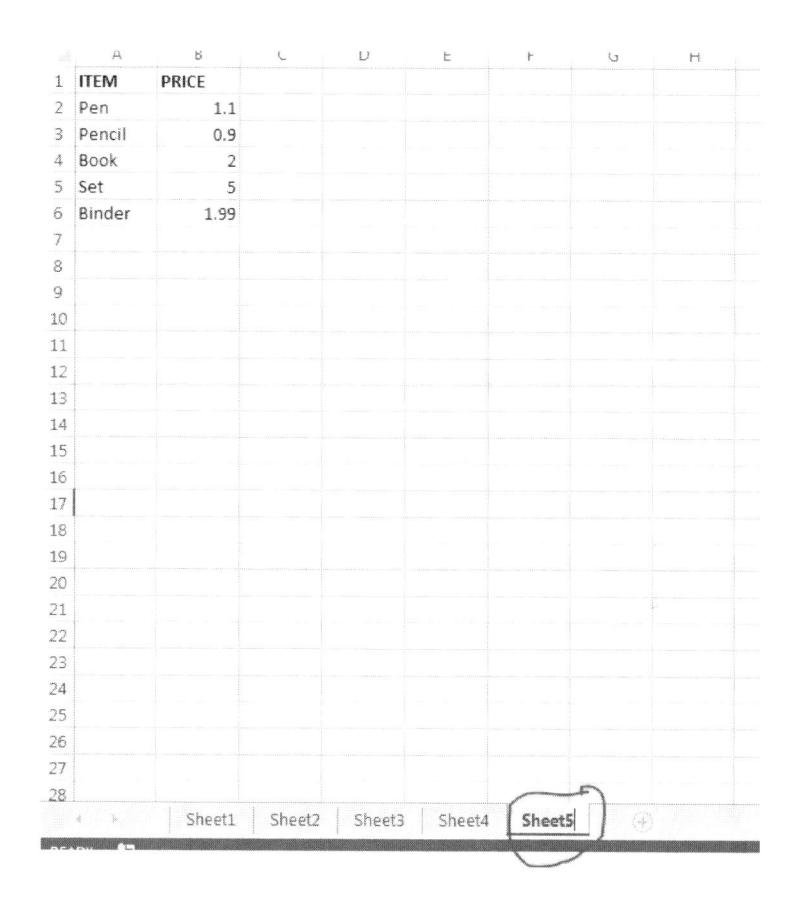

	A	B	C	D	E	F	G	H
1	ITEM	PRICE						
2	Pen	1.1						
3	Pencil	0.9						
4	Book	2						
5	Set	5						
6	Binder	1.99						

Sheet1 | Sheet2 | Sheet3 | Sheet4 | **Sheet5**

Hiding a Worksheet

To hide a worksheet, follow the steps given below:

1. Right the worksheet you need to hide then chooses the "Hide" option. The sheet will be hidden.

2. To unhide a worksheet, right click on any sheet name then choose the "Unhide…" option.

3. A dialog will be presented. Choose the worksheet that you need to unhide then click the "OK" button.

Deleting a Worksheet

Sometimes, you may need to delete a sheet that you no longer need. To delete a particular worksheet, follow the steps given below:

1. Right the name of the sheet you need to delete then choose "Delete".

2. If the sheet is empty, it will be deleted immediately, otherwise, you will see a confirmation dialog. Click the "Delete" button:

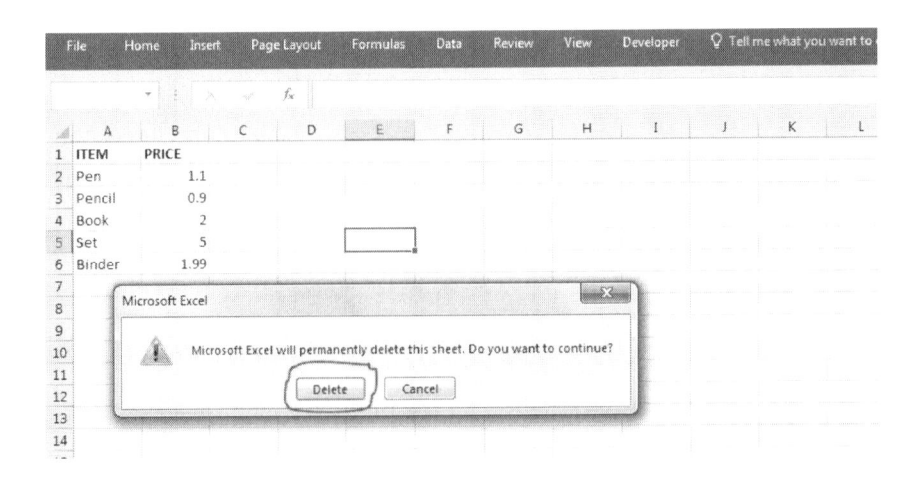

The worksheet will be deleted.

Inserting a Formula

The processing of entering formulas in Excel is done from the formula bar. The formula bar is shown below:

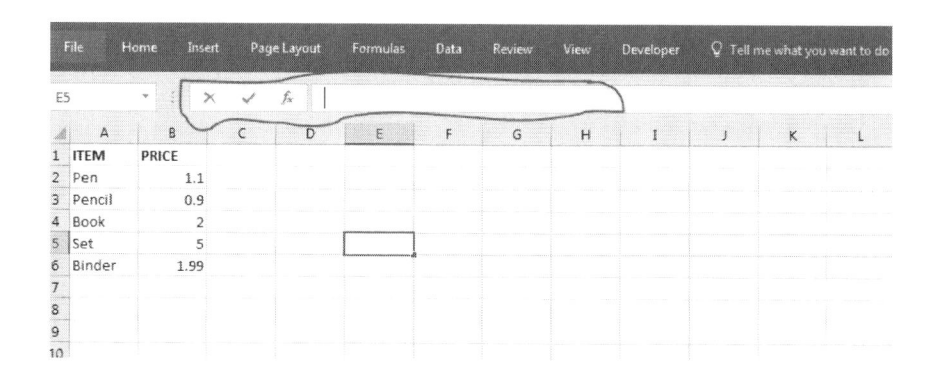

Consider the example given below:

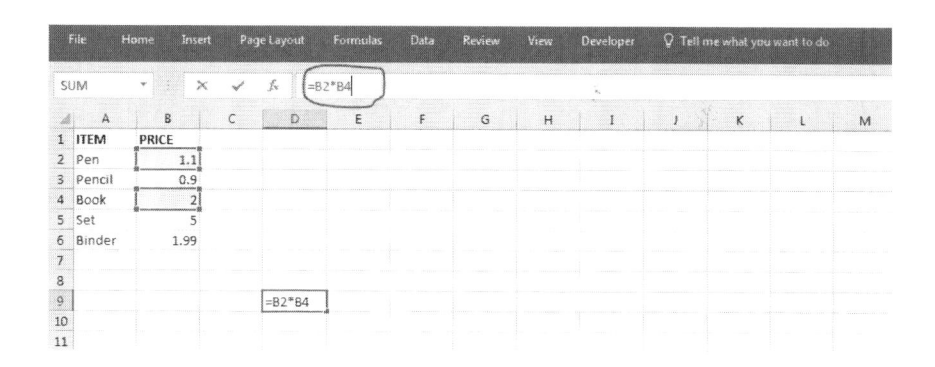

Once you have typed the formula, hit the enter key to get the results:

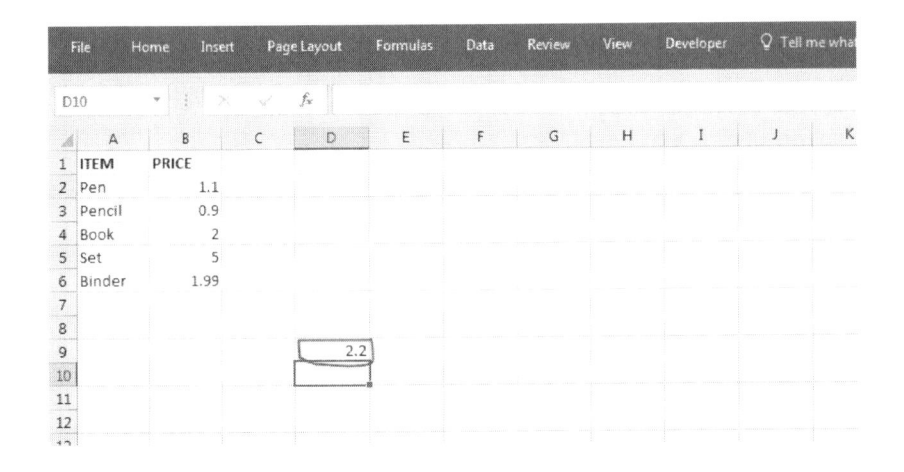

Any time that you need to change the contents of a particular cell, just highlight the cell, enter the new value then hit the enter key. You will see the changes have been made.

Deleting Data

There are various ways through which you can delete data on an Excel sheet. To delete the data through a mouse, just select or highlight the data to be deleted, right click it then choose the delete option:

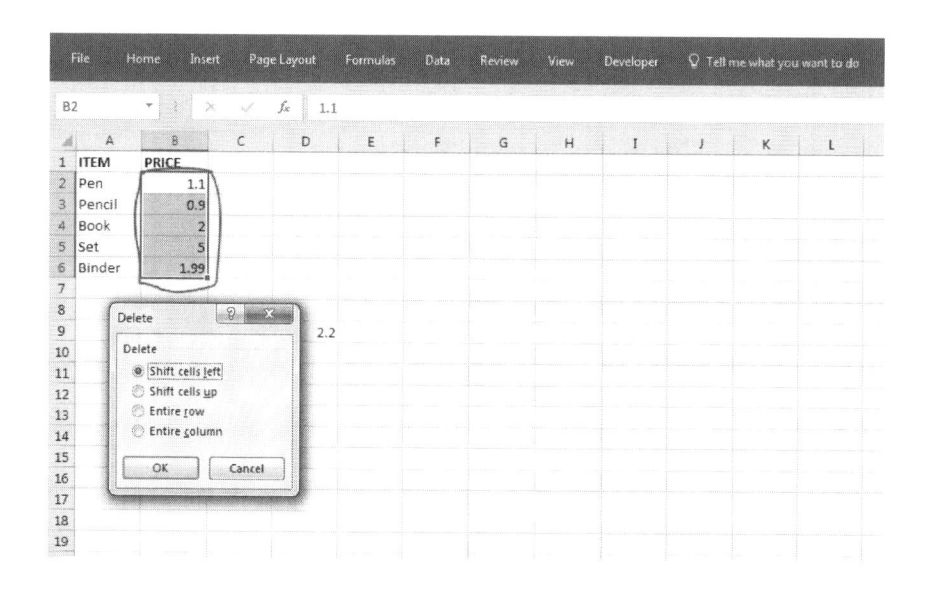

Choose the direction to which you need to shift the cells, and then click the "OK" button.

To delete data from the keyboard, just choose the data that you need to delete then hit the Delete key on the keyboard.

You can also choose the cells that you need to delete. To select them, use the mouse plus the control key. Right click on any option then choose the Delete option. The data will be deleted.

Moving Data

You can also move your data from one cell to another. To do this, highlight the data that you need to move. Right click it then choose the "Cut" option.

Click in the first cell where you need to move the data, right click it then choose the paste option.

Find & Replace

This is an Excel feature that can help you find what you are looking for. To get the Find & Replace dialogue, navigate through *Home → Find & Select → Find* or simply press the *Control + F Key*.

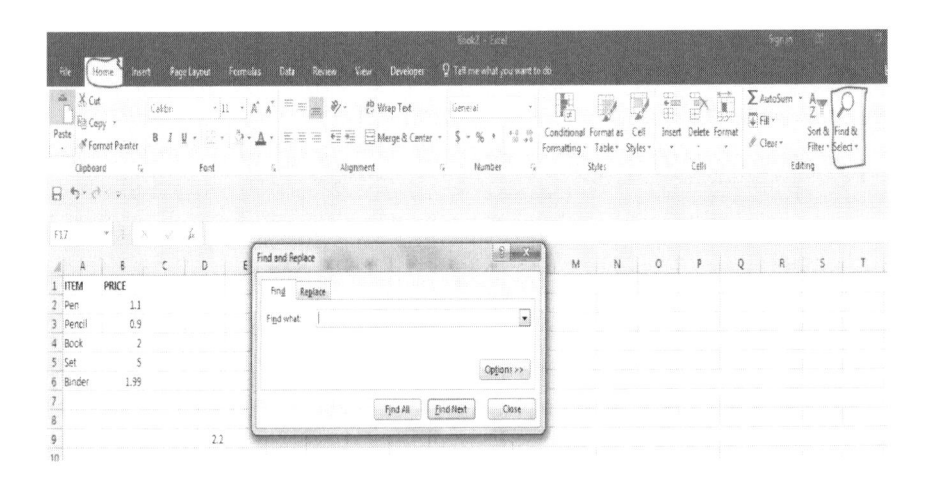

The Find & Replace dialogue will then be presented to you. You can type the text find in the Find tab and the text to replace within the Replace tab. For advanced searches such as when you need to consider the case the text to be searched is written in, click the "Options>>" button:

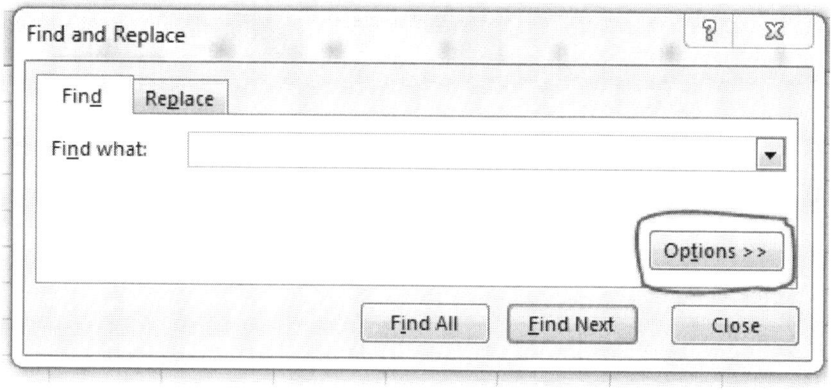
Find and Replace
Find
Replace
Find what:
Options >>
Find All
Find Next
Close

You can then activate the various options according to what you need for the search.

Adding Comments

Through comments, the purpose of a cell can be understood better. It can help a sheet user in knowing what is expected in a particular cell as well as for documentation purposes.

To add a comment to a particular cell, select the cell, click the Review tab then choose "New Comment":

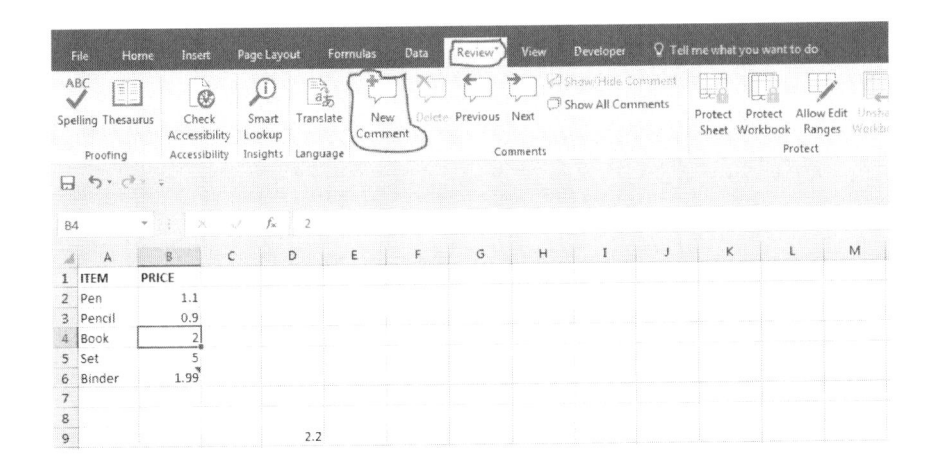

You can then type the comment in the text area that is provided. Anytime the user points the cell, they will see the comment.

To edit or change the comment, click the cell whose comment you need to edit. On the top bar, click "Review" then choose "Edit Comment".

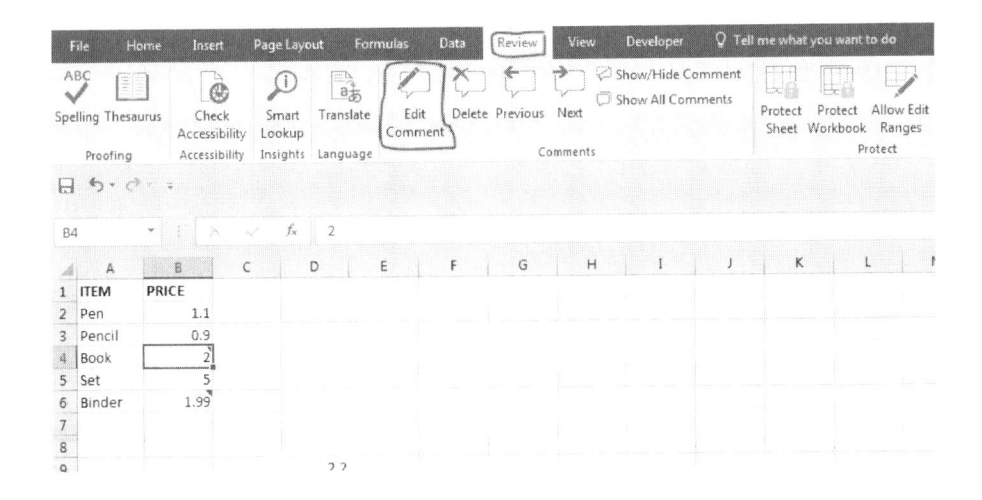

Once you have edited the comment, just click outside its cell and it will be saved.

It is also possible for you to format the comment and change various attributes of the same like the font type, font size, color etc. To do this, click the cell, from the Review tab choose "Edit Comment". Select the comment then right click it. Choose "Format Comment…"

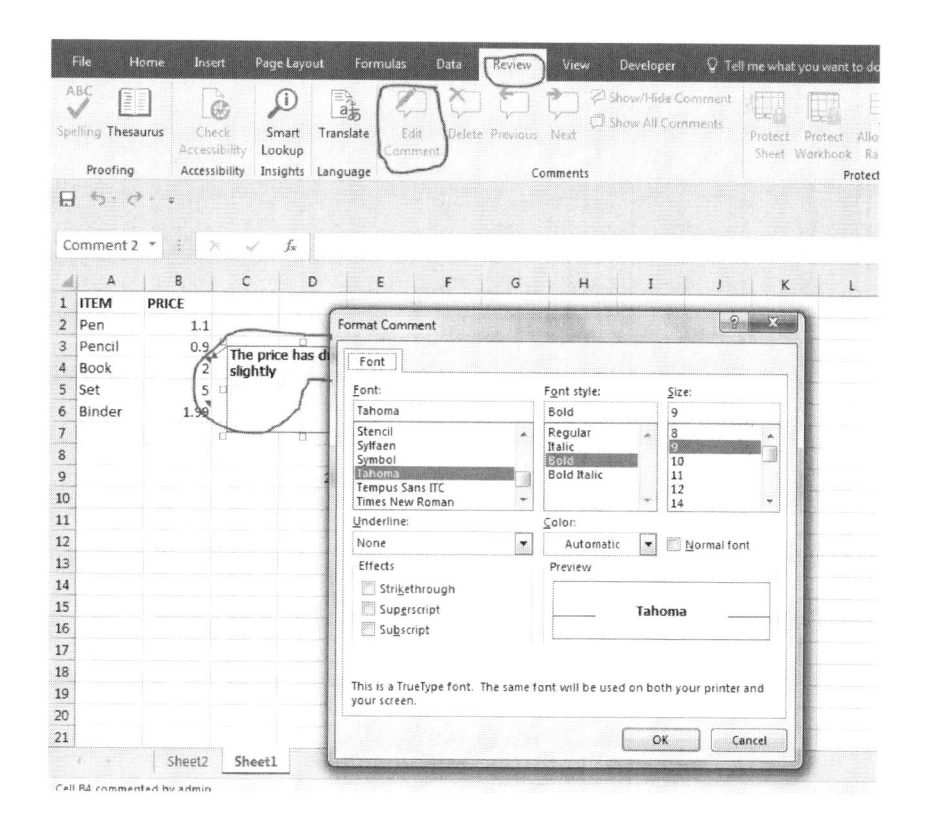

You can then change the various properties of the comment and once done, click the "OK" button.

Adding a Text Box

Text boxes are graphic objects combining text with rectangular graphic object. Text boxes and cell comments normally show text in rectangular box. With cell comments, the text is shown when the cell is selected but the text box always shows the text.

To add a text box, click on Insert tab, click Text on the top right corner of the excel sheet. You will see a dropdown from which you should choose a text box. You can then draw the text box by dragging the mouse cursor then add a text to the text box:

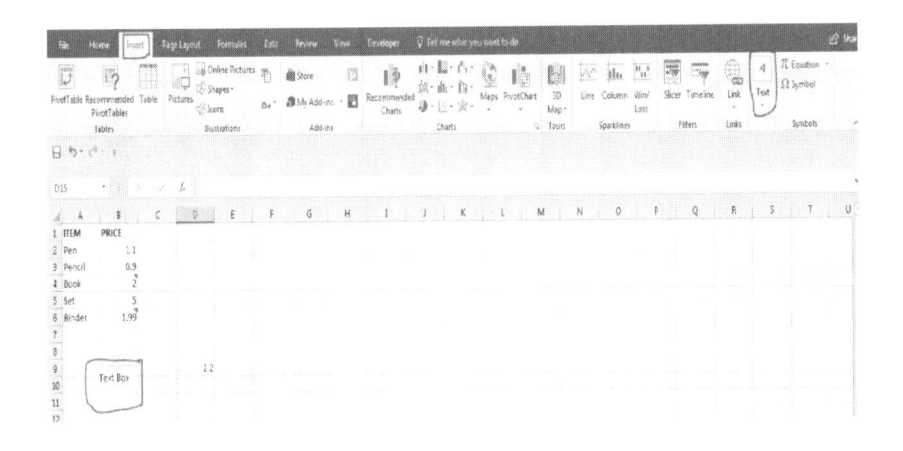

Once you have added the text box, it will be possible for you to change the various properties of its text and even format the shape of the text box.

Chapter 3- Formatting Cells

Cell Type

An Excel cell can be used for holding data of different types including Numbers, Currency, Dates and others. You can set the cell to be of type of the data you expect to be added to the cell.

To do this, click inside the cell you need to set, right click it, choose "Format Cells..." In the next window dialog, click the tab for Number on the left.

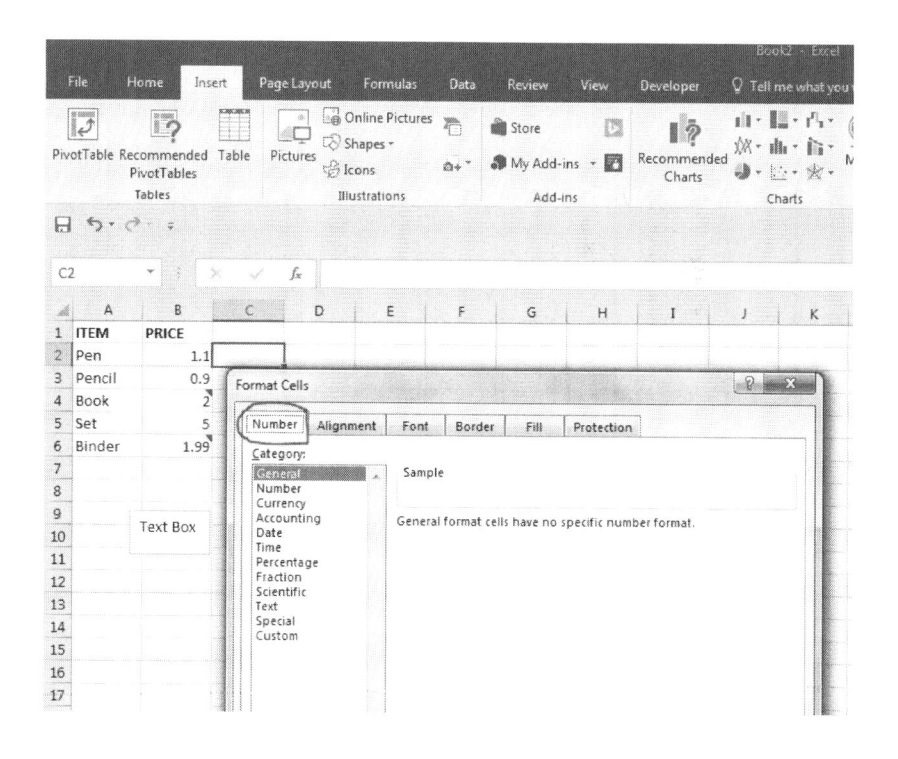

Choose the type from the list of the available types then click the OK button.

That is it. If you have chosen date for example, the value you add to the cell will be converted into a date.

Rotating Cells

It is possible for you to change the orientation of a cell by rotating it by a certain degree. To do this, first click on the cell whose text you need to orient. Click the Home tab then click the Orientation icon. Choose the way in which you need to display the text for the cell:

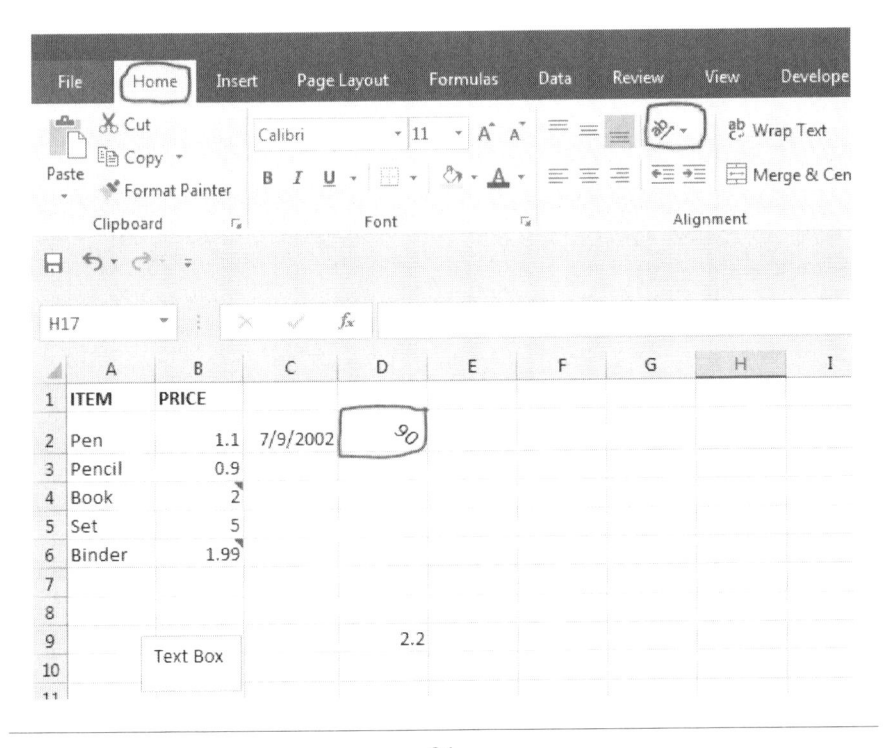

As you can see above, the text 90 has been rotated in a clockwise direction. There are numerous ways of orienting the text, so the choice is yours.

Other than doing the orientation on the text for the cell, it is possible for you to add the orientation feature to the cell itself and any text added to it will be oriented in that direction. This can be done by following the steps given below:

Click inside the cell for which you need to set the oriented, right click it then choose "Format Cells…" A new dialog wills popup. Click the "Alignment" tab on this dialog. On the bottom right of the dialog, you will be able to set the number of degrees by which you need to orient the text as shown below:

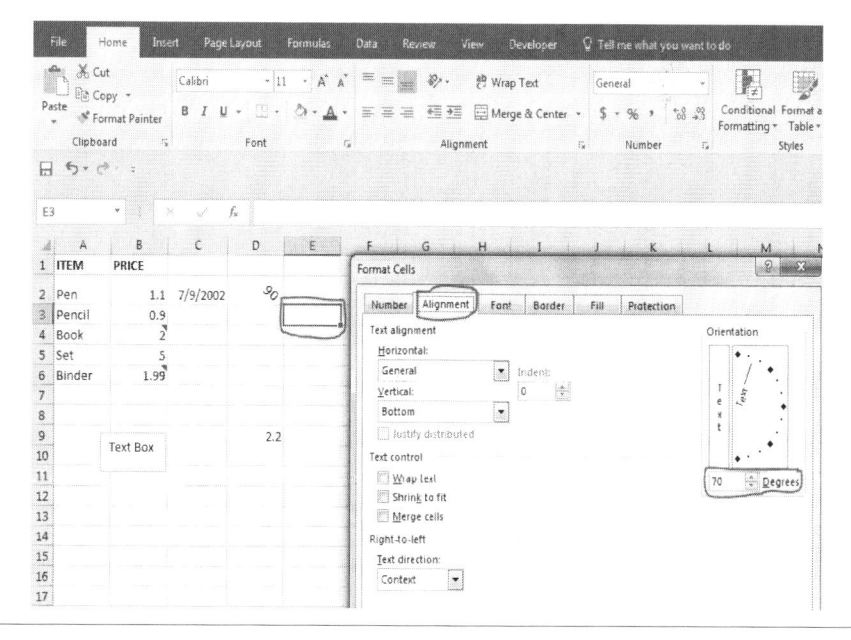

As shown in the above screenshot, I have set the orientation to 70 degrees for the cell. Once done, click the OK button located at the bottom. You will be done.

Once you add text to the cell for whose orientation you have set, you will notice that it will be orientated by the number of degrees that you have set as shown below:

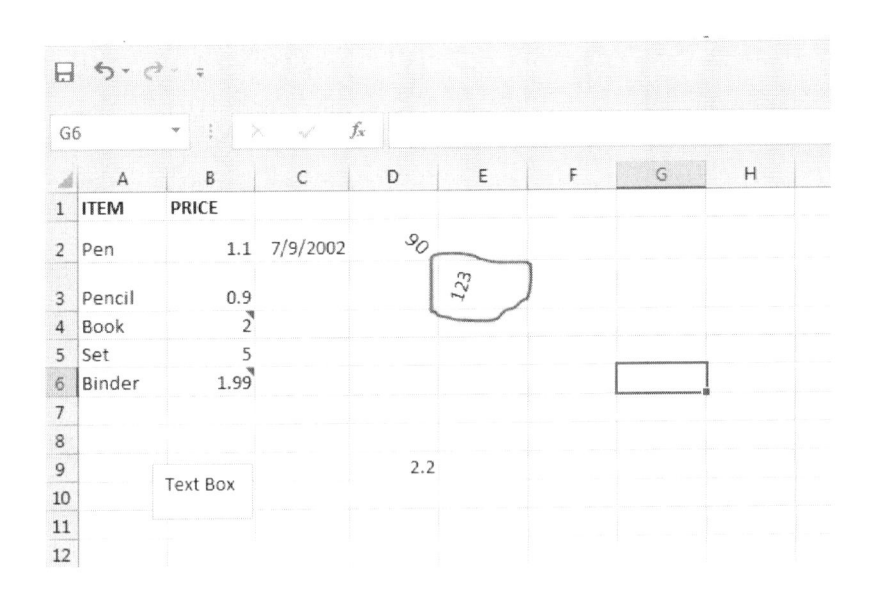

That is how the text is aligned.

Changing Background Color

In MS Excel, each cell a default background color of white.

However, it is possible for you to change this to what you need. To do this, you need to navigate through *Home tab -> Font group -> Background color.*

To change the color, select the cell or cells whose color needs to be changed. Click the Home tab, and then choose a color from the color group as shown below:

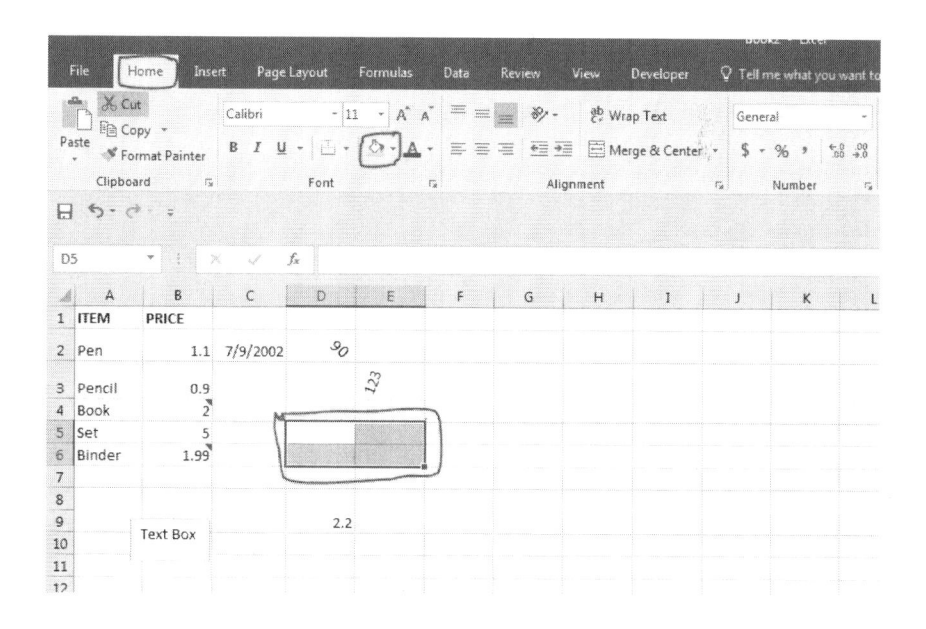

Once you begin to type text in the cells whose background color you have formatted, the background color you have chosen will not be changed.

Changing Foreground Color

In MS Excel, the default text or foreground color is black. This color can be changed from the Home tab by following the steps given below:

Just select the cell or cells for which you need to set the text color. Click the Home tab then choose the color from the group of colors provided:

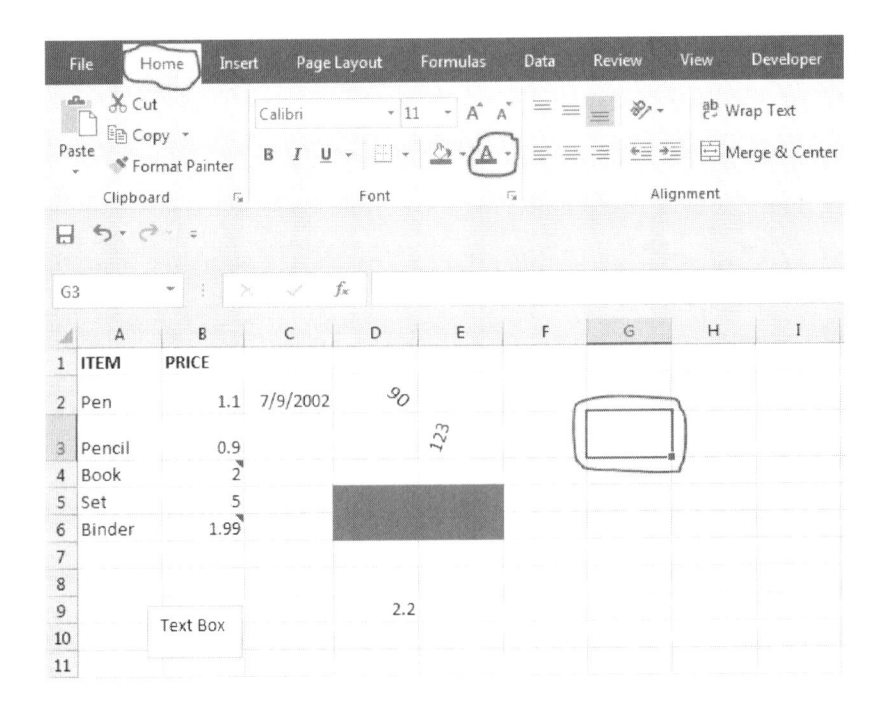

When you begin to type the text in the cell or cells, you will notice that it uses the color you have chosen for the cells.

Merge and Wrap

With MS Excel, it is possible for you to merge one or more cells. After merging the cells, their contents are not combined. You only combine a group of cells into a single cell occupying a similar space.

There are various ways through which you can merge cells in Excel. You can use the "Merge & Center" option which can be found under Home tab. This can be used as follows:

Select the cells that you need to merge. Click the Home tab then choose "Merge & Center" as shown below:

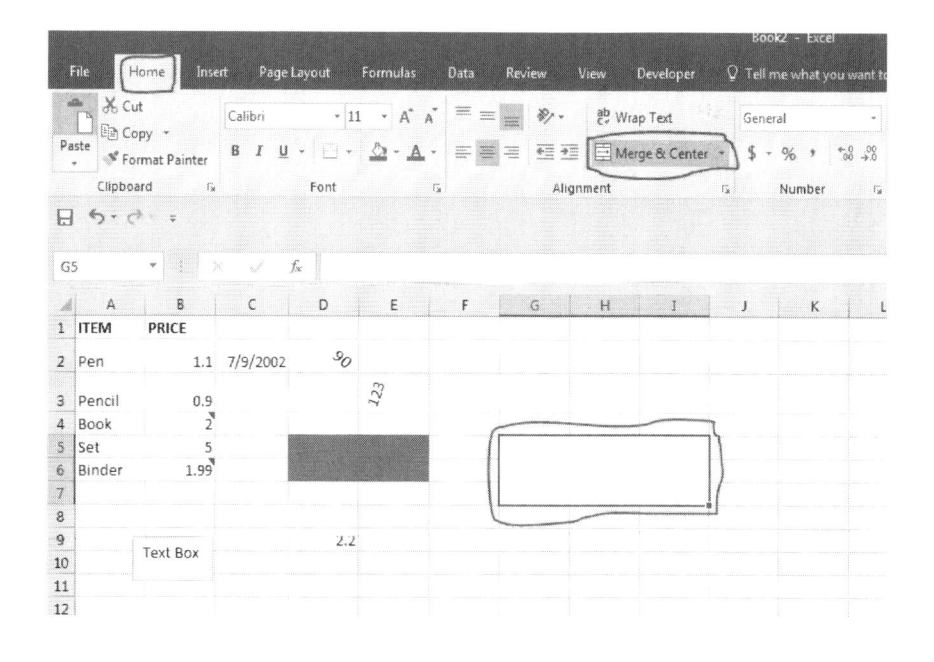

As shown above, the cells have been merged together and they can be used as one cell.

You can also achieve the same by selecting the cells to be merged, right clicking them and choosing "Format Cells…" In the dialog box that appears, click the "Alignment" tab. You can then click the checkbox for "Merge cells" then click the "OK" button:

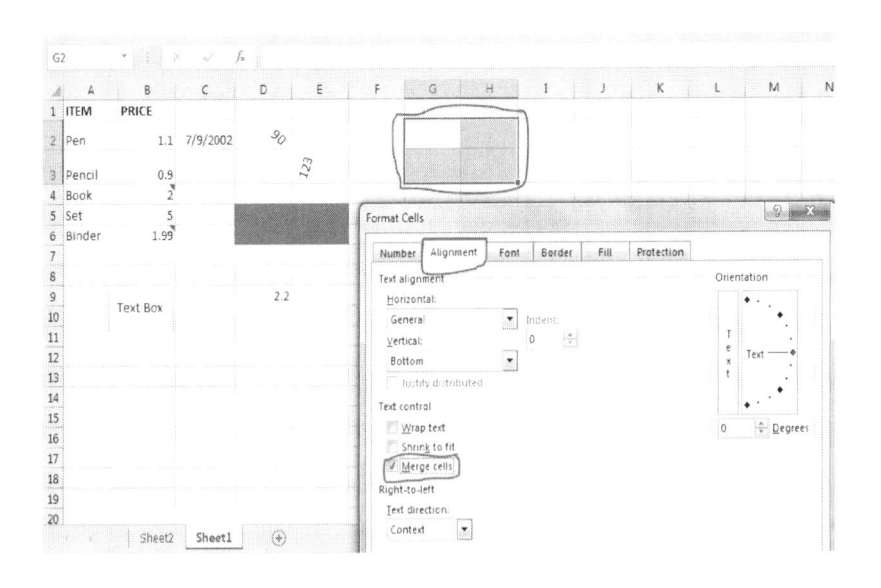

Once you click the OK button, the highlighted cells will be merged.

Sometimes, the text that you add to a particular cell may exceed or fail to fit in a cell. In such a case, we recommend that you wrap the text so that it fits into the cell. You can also shrink the text and it will fit well into the cell.

Suppose that we have the following text in an Excel cell:

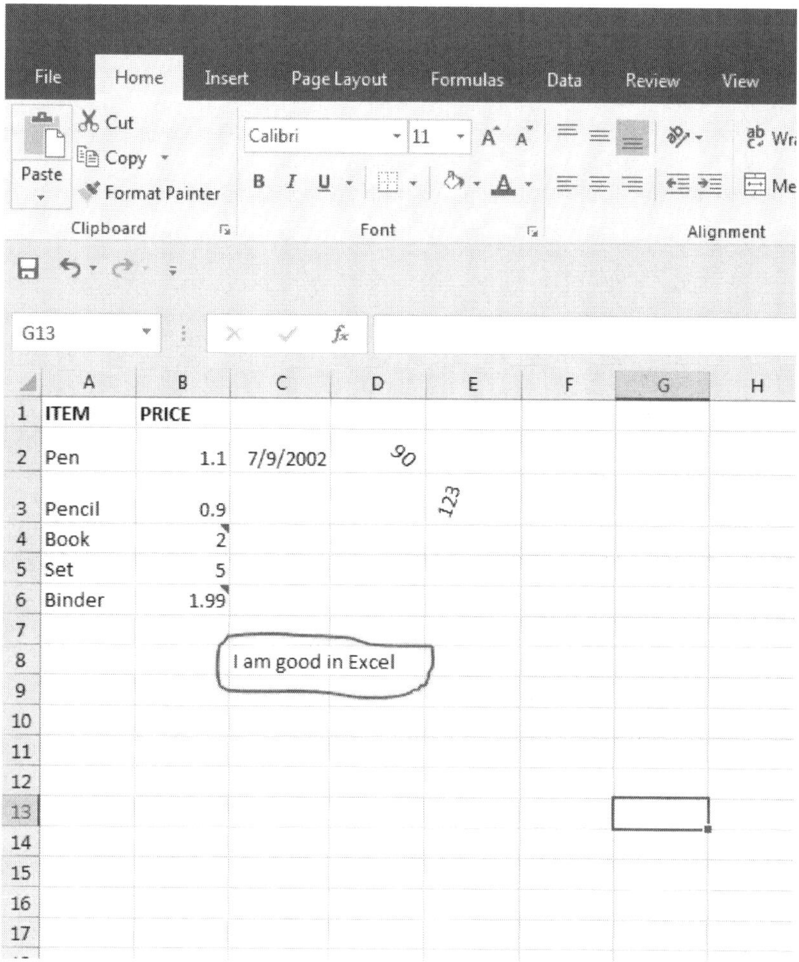
File
Home
Insert
Page Layout
Formulas
Data
Review
View
Cut
Copy
Paste
Format Painter
Clipboard
Calibri
11
B I U
Font
Alignment
G13
A
B
C
D
E
F
G
H
ITEM
PRICE
Pen
1.1
7/9/2002
90
123
Pencil
0.9
Book
2
Set
5
Binder
1.99
I am good in Excel

As shown above, the text spans more than one cell. Our goal is to have it fit into one cell. This can be done by use of the "Wrap text" feature as follows:

Right click the cell with text. This is cell where you began to write the text. Choose "Format Cells..." In the dialog box that appears, click the Alignment tab then click the checkbox for "Wrap text" as shown below:

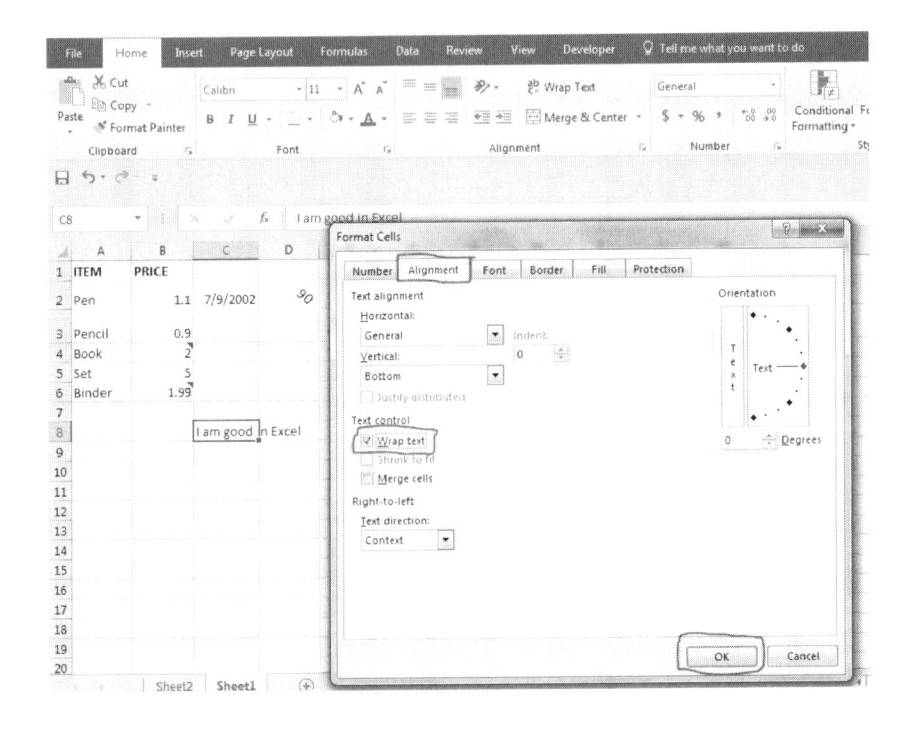

After clicking the checkbox, click the OK button. The text will then be wrapped and you will see it change structure to the following:

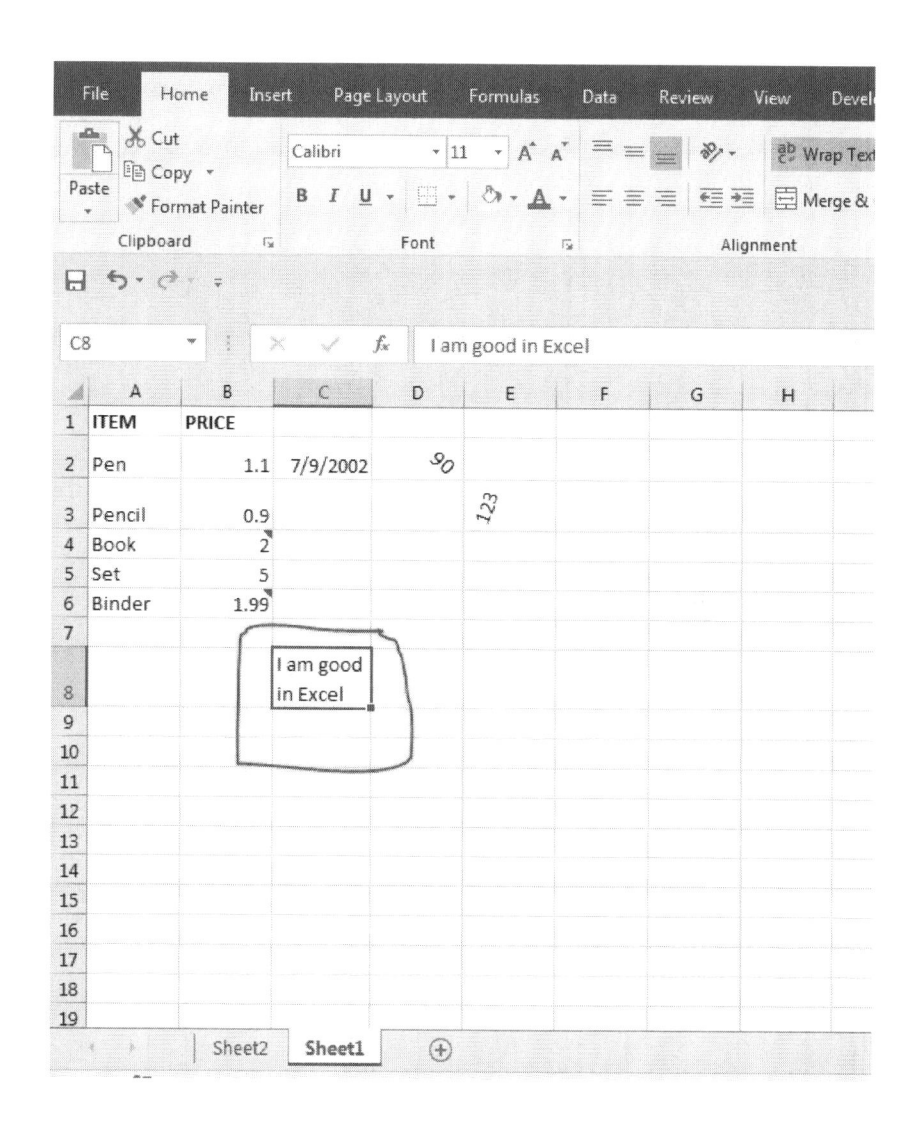

Now, the text is in a single cell unlike previously when it spanned multiple cells.

Assuming that you have the same text that spans more than one cells. Instead of wrapping it, you can choose to shrink it to fit into the cell.

To do this, just right click the cell with the text, then choose "Format Cells..." In the dialog that appears, click the "Alignment" tab then click the checkbox for "Shrink to fit". Once done, click the OK button and observe what happens to the text:

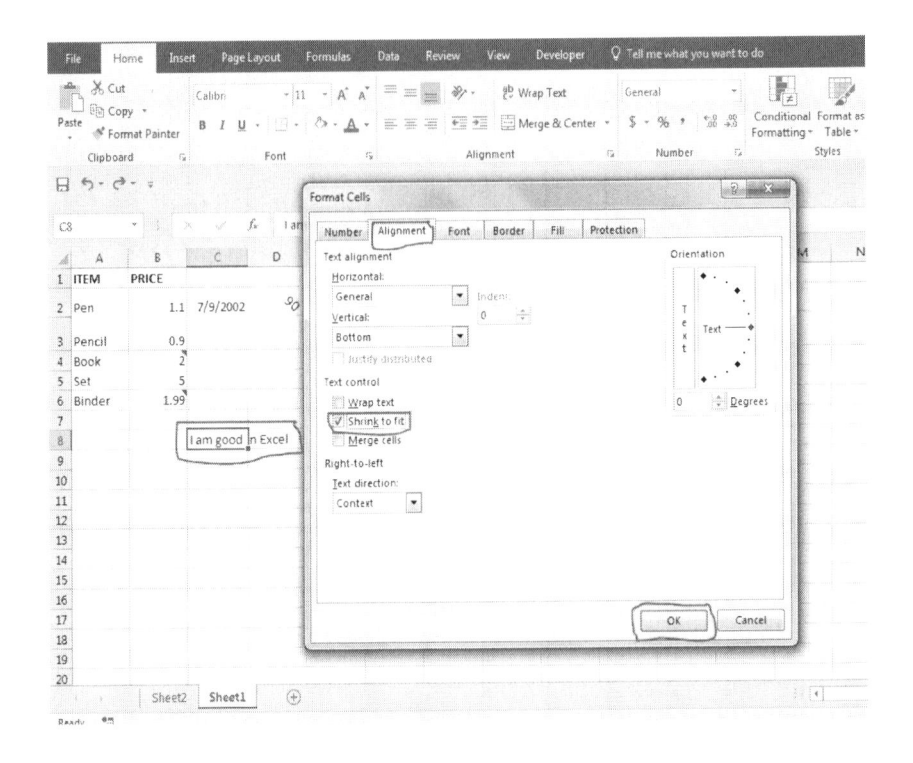

You will notice that the text will be shrinking to fit into the space within the cell as shown below:

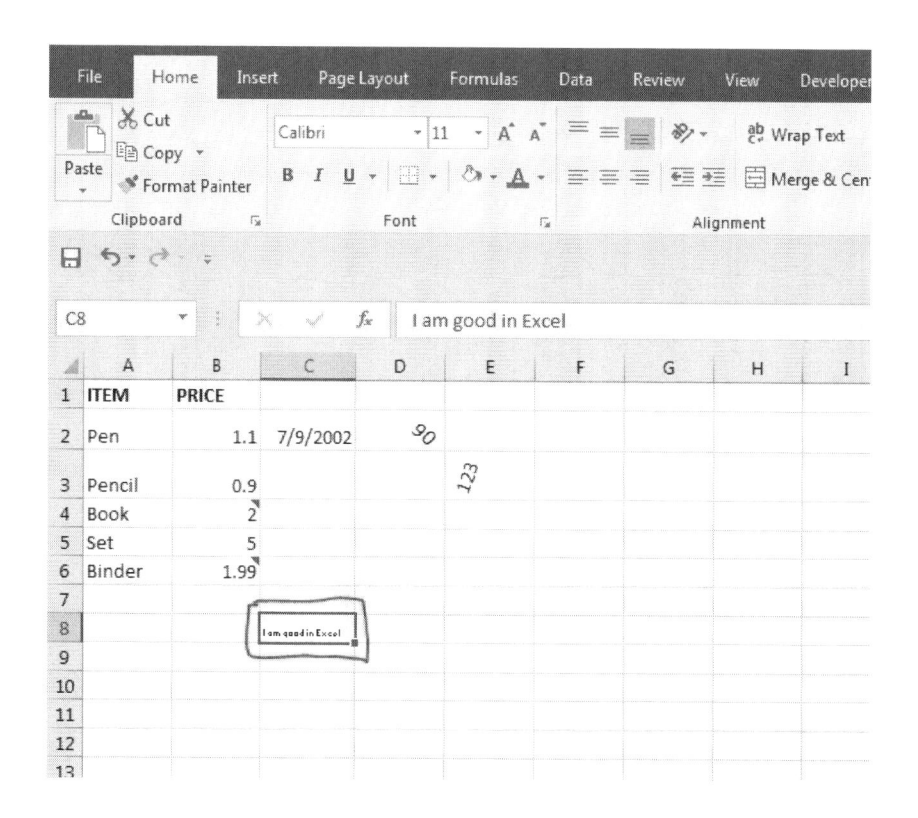

However, as you can see above, the text is not readable due to its small size. This option, that is, Shrink to fit, may not be the best for you. Of course, it will be determined by the length of the text added to the cell. If the text is not that longer, it may fit into the space of the cell.

Borders and Shades

With MS Excel, you can add borders to your cells. The border can be applied to not only one cell, but a group of cells. To apply this, just select the cells for which you need to apply the border.

Right click the selected cells then click "Format Cells..." Click the "Border" tab, choose the type of border you will want to use then click the OK button:

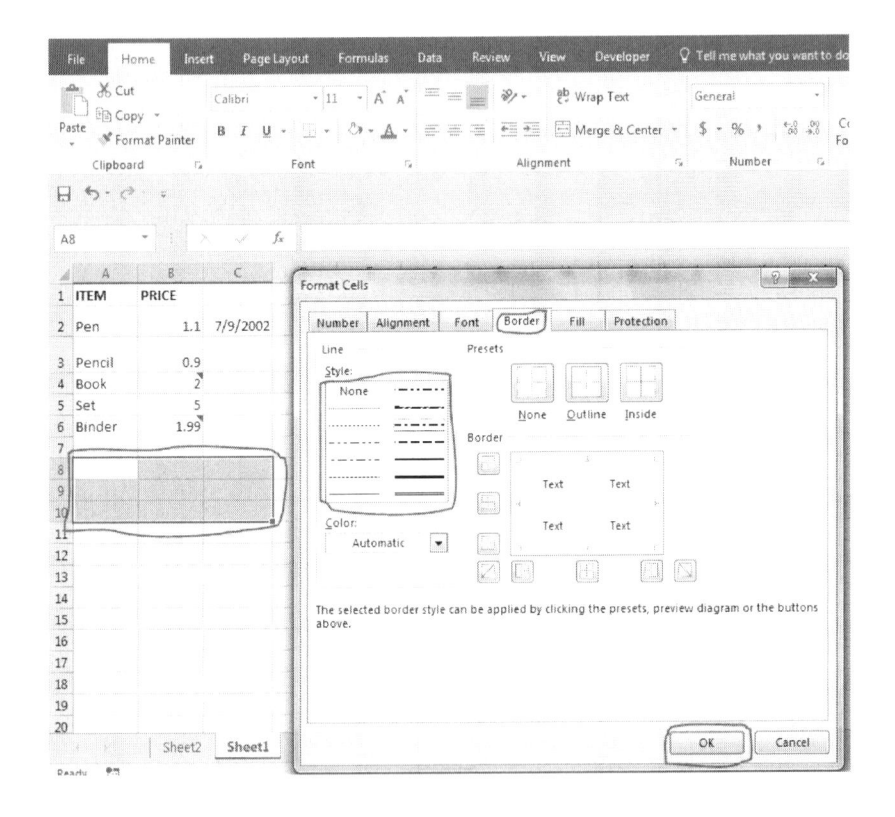

You can also choose the border color if you wish to use one. To apply the borders, you can click the Home tab, Font Group then choose the border you need.

Chapter 4- Arithmetic Operations

Excel provides you with an easy way of carrying out arithmetic operations. These operations include multiplication, addition, subtraction and division. Suppose we have the following data in an Excel sheet:

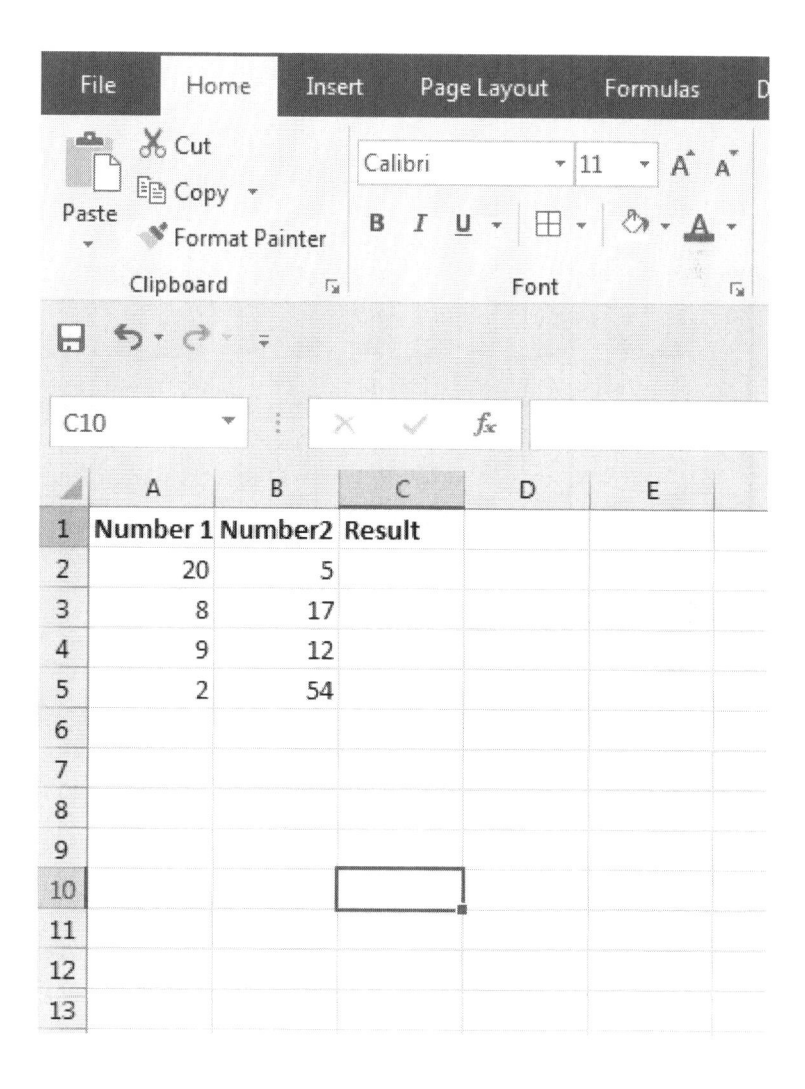

	A	B	C
1	Number 1	Number2	Result
2	20	5	
3	8	17	
4	9	12	
5	2	54	

We can now use arithmetic operators to carry out calculations that we need. To perform calculations in Excel, one should begin with the equal sign (=). We then specify the cells whose values are to be involved in the arithmetic operations, and the cell names are separated using the colon operator. In the above sheet, get the sum of values in cells A2 and B2, we use the following formula:

=A2+B2

If I type the formula then I press the enter key, I get the result:

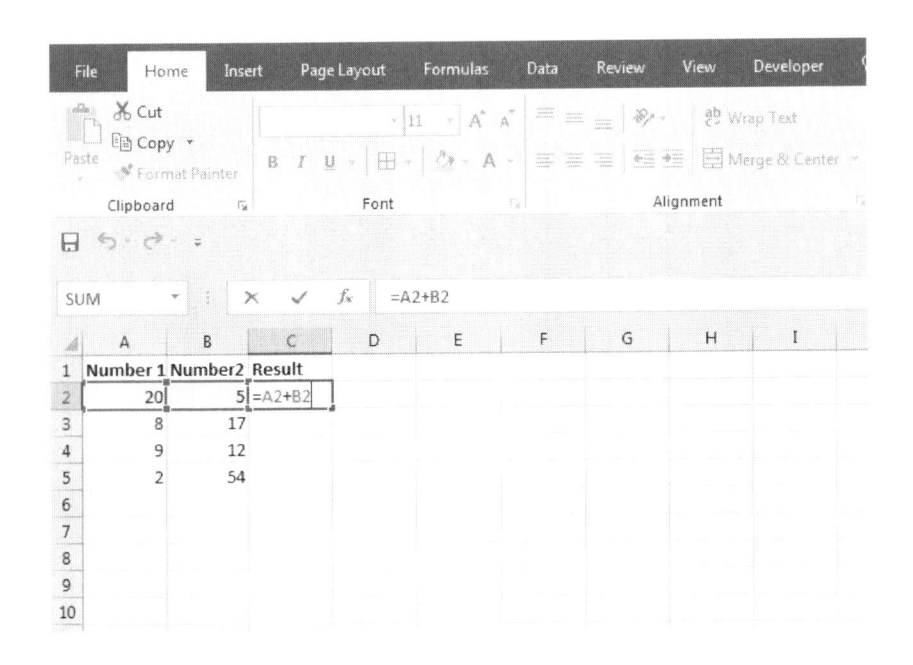

The result should be shown as follows:

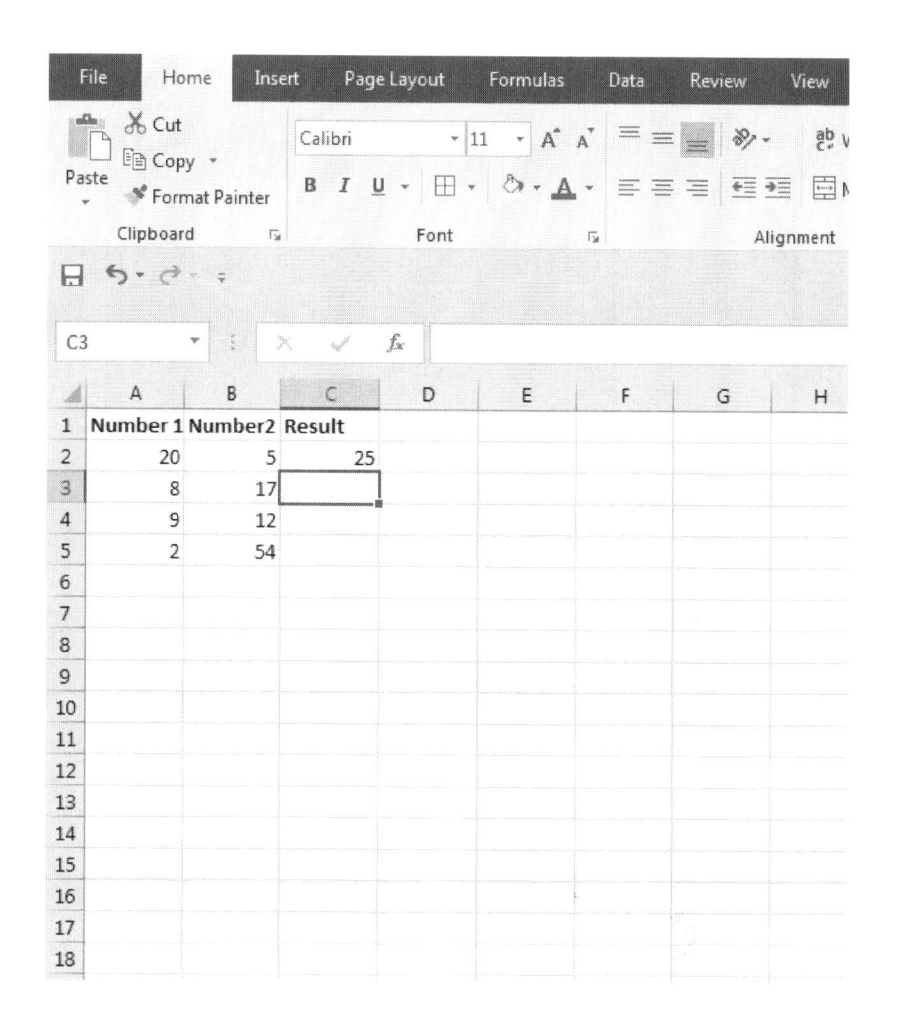

For subtraction, we will use the minus (-) sign to get the difference between cells A3 and B3. This can be done with the following formula:

=A3-B3

The formulas for multiplication and division will be as follows respectively:

=A4*B4
=A5/B5

The operations then give us the results given below:

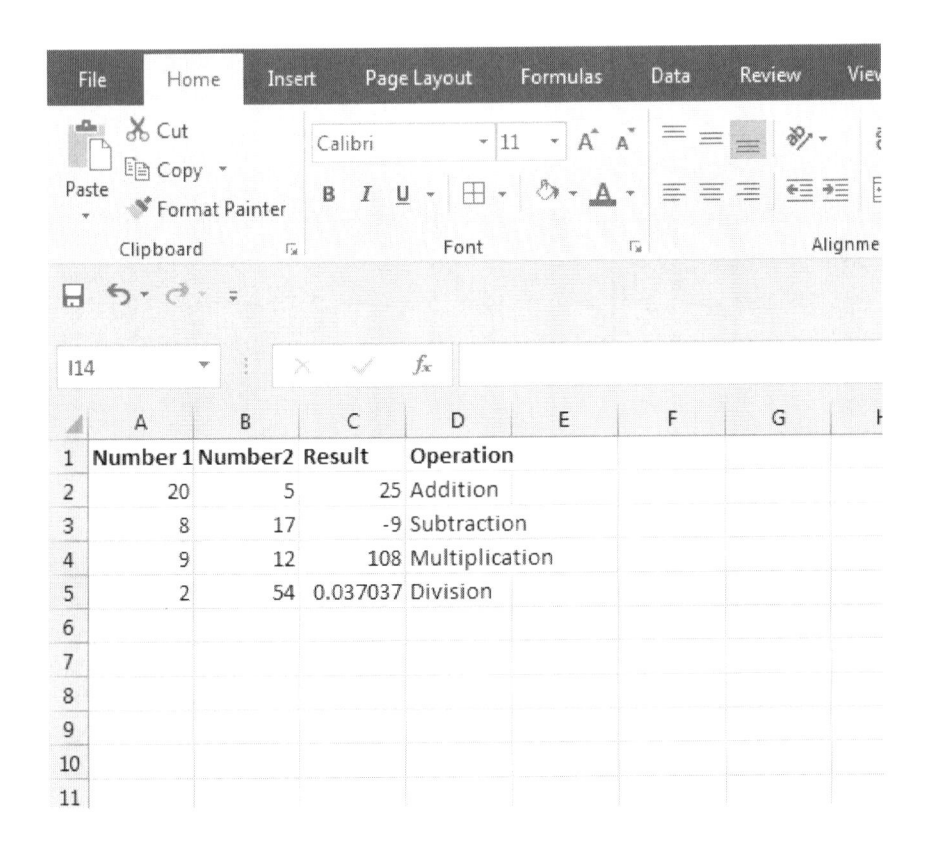

	A	B	C	D
1	Number 1	Number2	Result	Operation
2	20	5	25	Addition
3	8	17	-9	Subtraction
4	9	12	108	Multiplication
5	2	54	0.037037	Division

That is how we can perform arithmetic operations in Excel. You must know the operator associated with each operation. You should also know how to number the cells.

Chapter 5- Validating, Grouping and Filters

Validation

Data validation in Excel helps us to avoid the mistakes that are avoidable. With this feature, one is able to set some rules that must be followed when one is entering data into a cell. Example, you can create a validation rule that requires the user to enter only whole numbers ranging between 0 and 10 into a particular cell. If the user deviates from this rule, you can inform them by displaying a message.

For you to specify the type of data that will be allowed into a particular field, follow the steps given below:

Select the range or cell.

Navigate by clicking through *Data -> Data Tools -> Data Validation.*

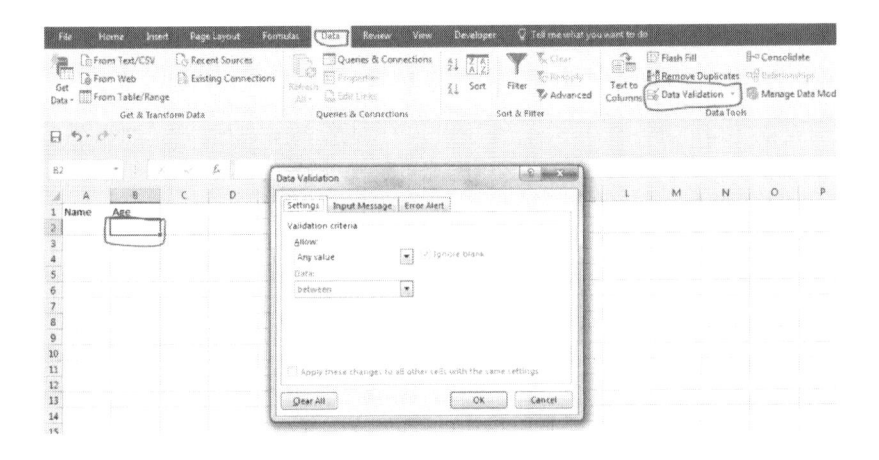

A new dialog box appears with three tabs namely *Settings, Input Message* and *Error Alert*.

The Settings tab allows you to set the validation that you need. You can specify the type of data that you expect to be entered into the cell by selecting one option from the "Allow" drop down. If you choose "Any Value" on this drop down, then no data validation will be implemented on the cell. Since in this case we are validating a cell for age, it must be a whole number. After choosing the whole number option, we are allowed to choose both the minimum and maximum value to be allowed into the cell.

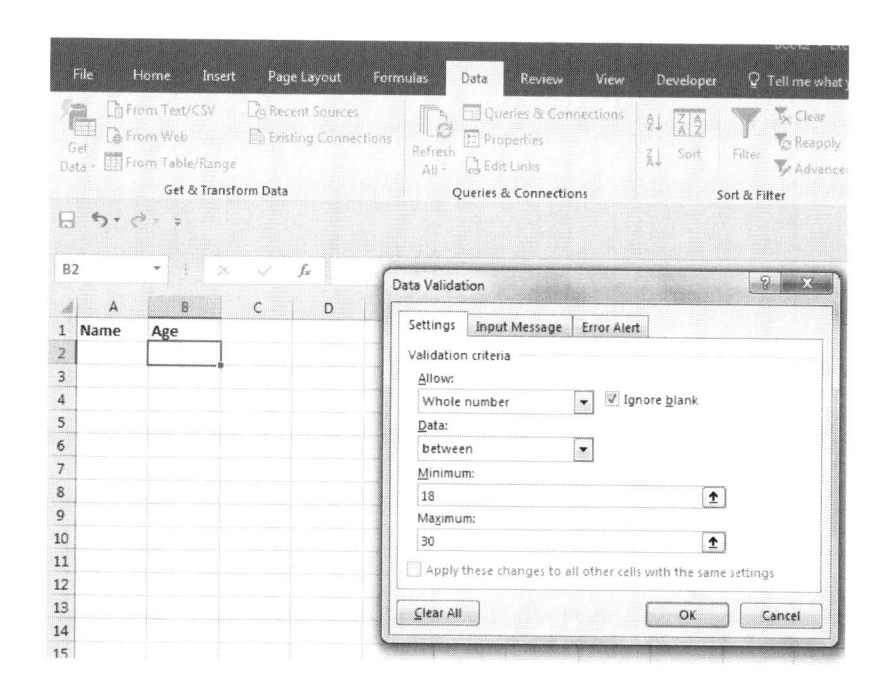

In the above case, I have specified that the value for the cell should range between 18 and 30. Once done with the specification, you should click the OK button and the changes will be applied.

To see whether this is working correctly, let us enter a value that meets the criteria specified above then insert a value that violates the criteria in the cell:

If we enter a value like 80, we get the following error message:

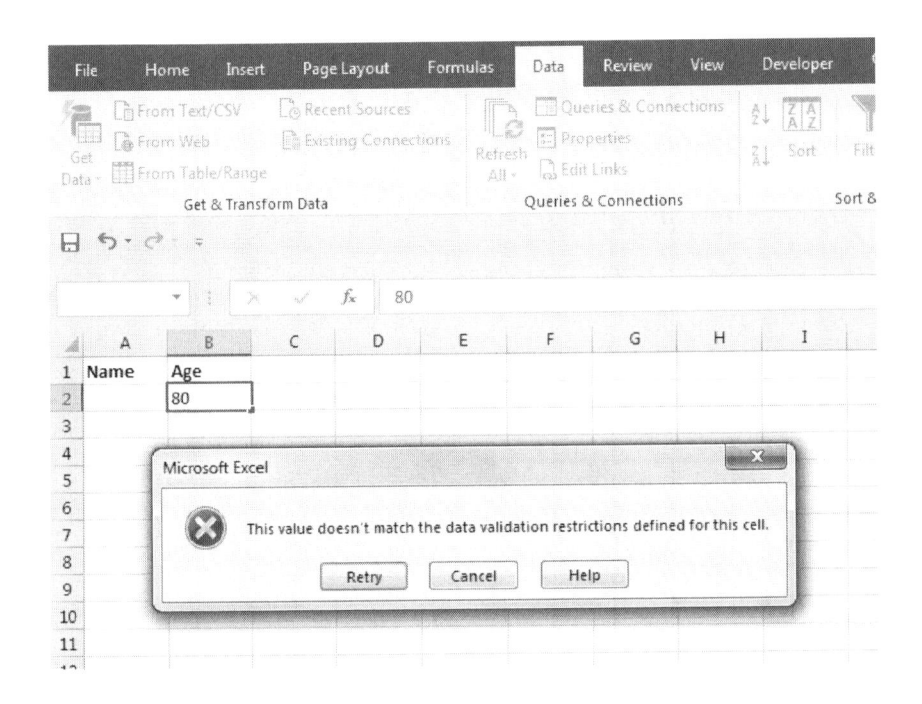

This shows that we have violated the criteria. What o we enter a value that meets the criteria:

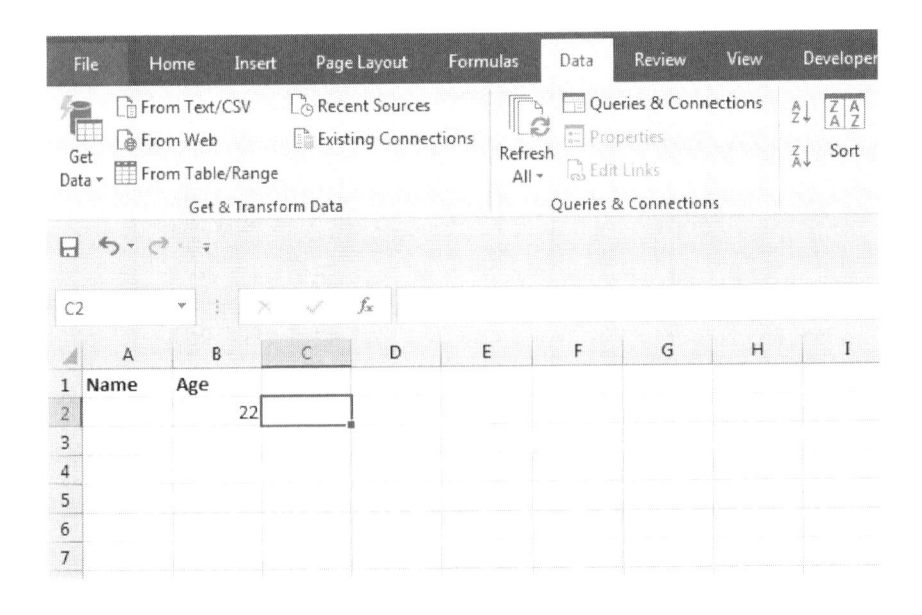

44

There is no problem with that. In the *Input Message* tab, you can specify the message that will be presented to the user whenever they choose the cell. You must enter the title and the message to be shown.

In the Error Alert tab, you are allowed to specify an error message. Again, you must enter the title as well as the message itself. This message will be shown once you enter a wrong value into the cell. In my case, I specify the following error message:

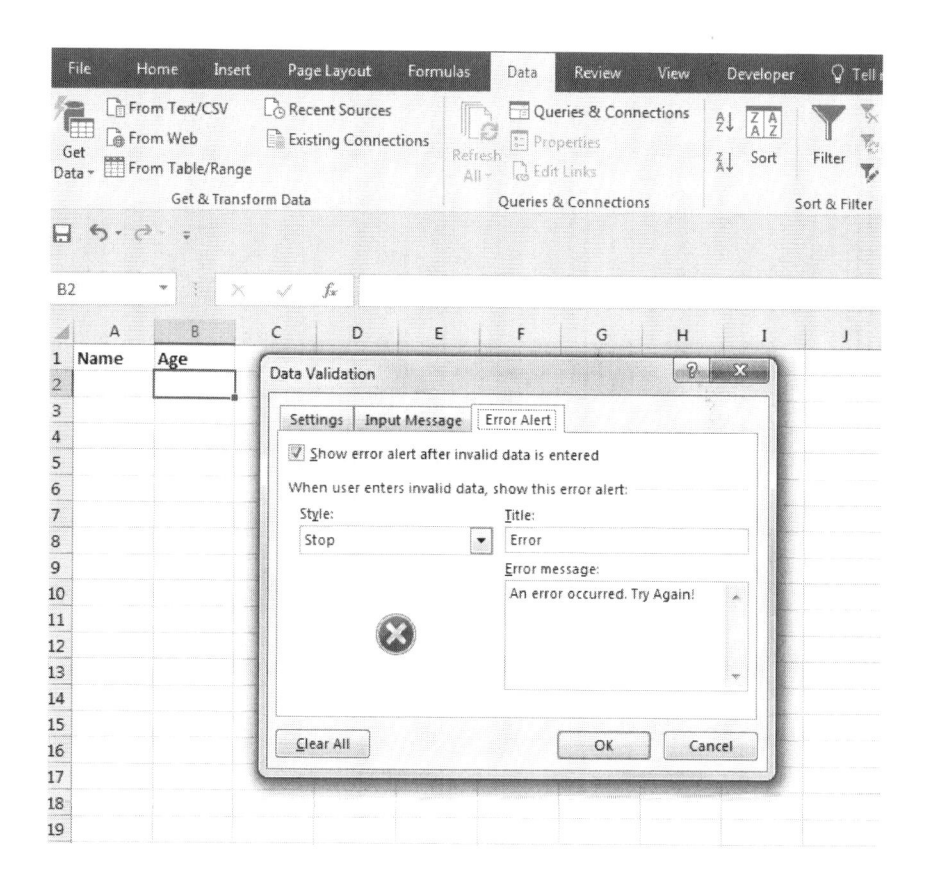

If I enter a wrong value, the error message will be shown as follows:

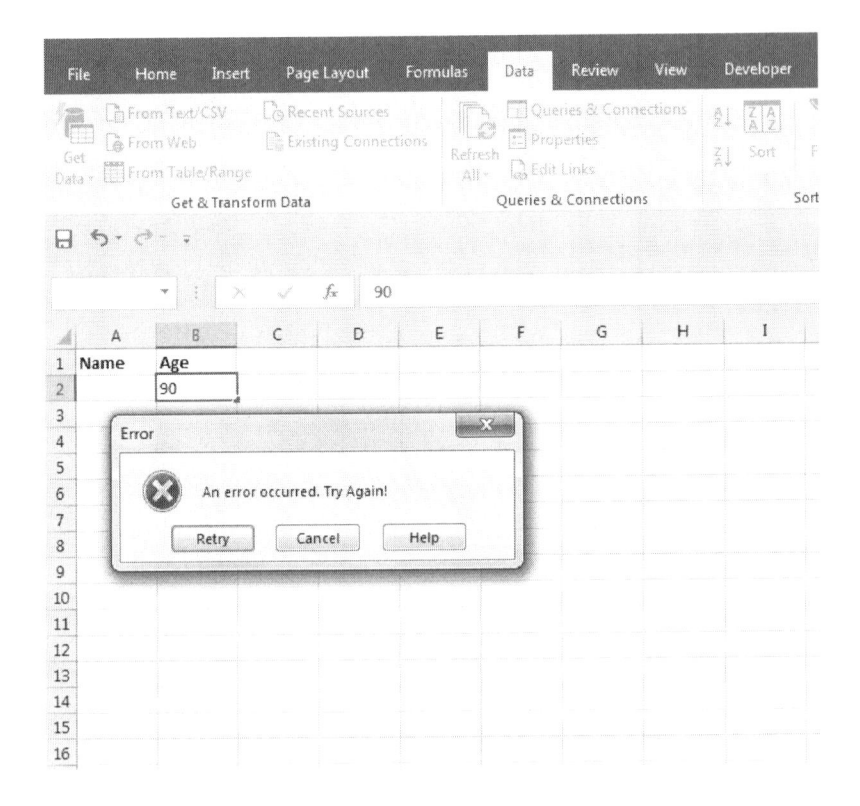

Data Filters

With data filters in Excel, we can get the data that matches our desired criteria. In short, they are used for filtering data. You can use filters to know the names of employees whose names begin with "N", or the name of employees whose salaries less, greater than or equal to a particular amount.

Suppose we have an excel sheet showing the names of students and their ages:

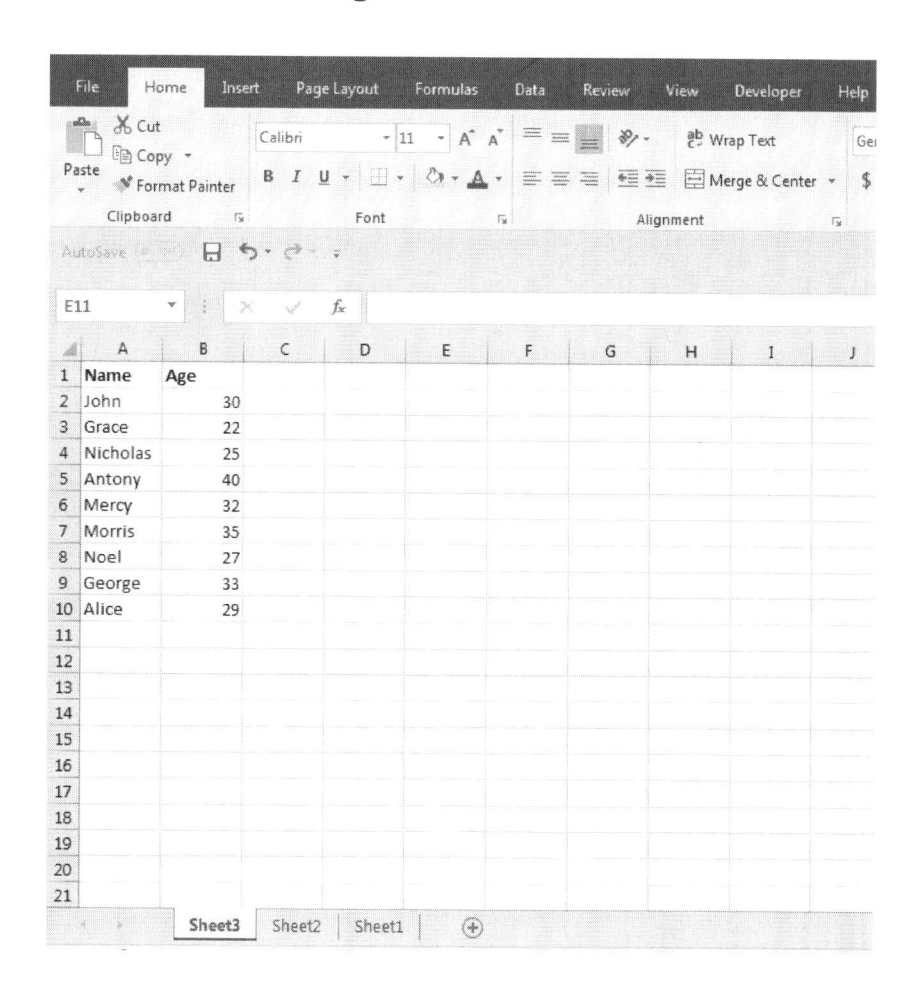

	A	B
1	Name	Age
2	John	30
3	Grace	22
4	Nicholas	25
5	Antony	40
6	Mercy	32
7	Morris	35
8	Noel	27
9	George	33
10	Alice	29

Now that you have the above data in a sheet, select the two columns, that is, Name and Age. Next, click the Data tab then click Sort & Filter.

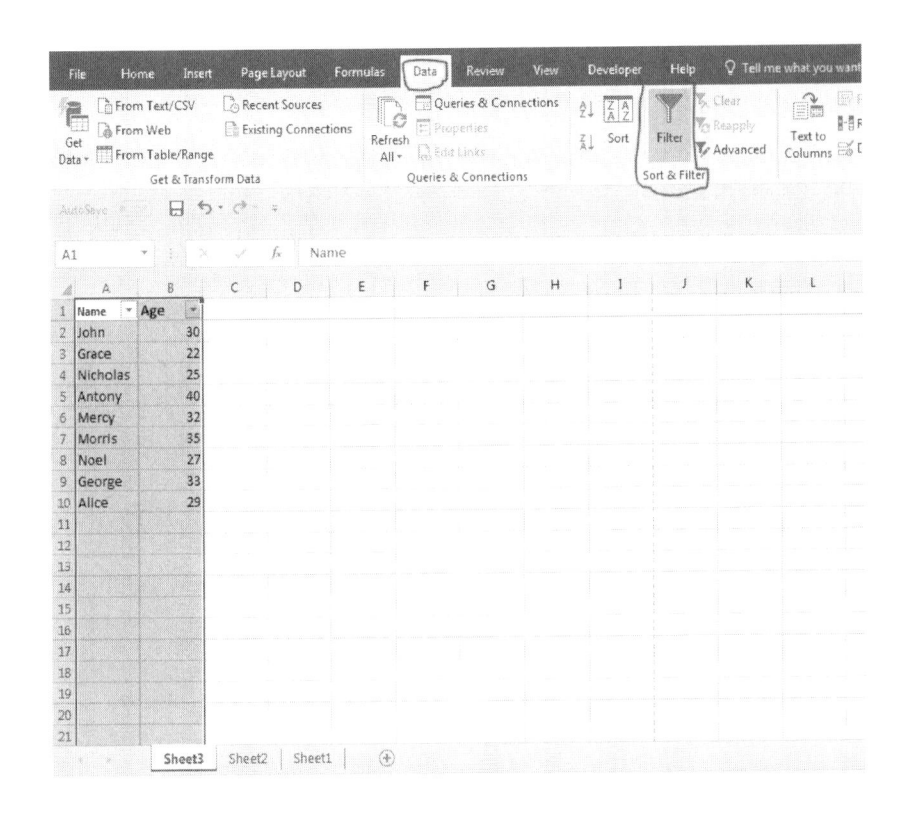

Click the drop-down arrow that appears on the right of Name filter, click on "Text Filters", then click "Begins With..." A new window sill pops up:

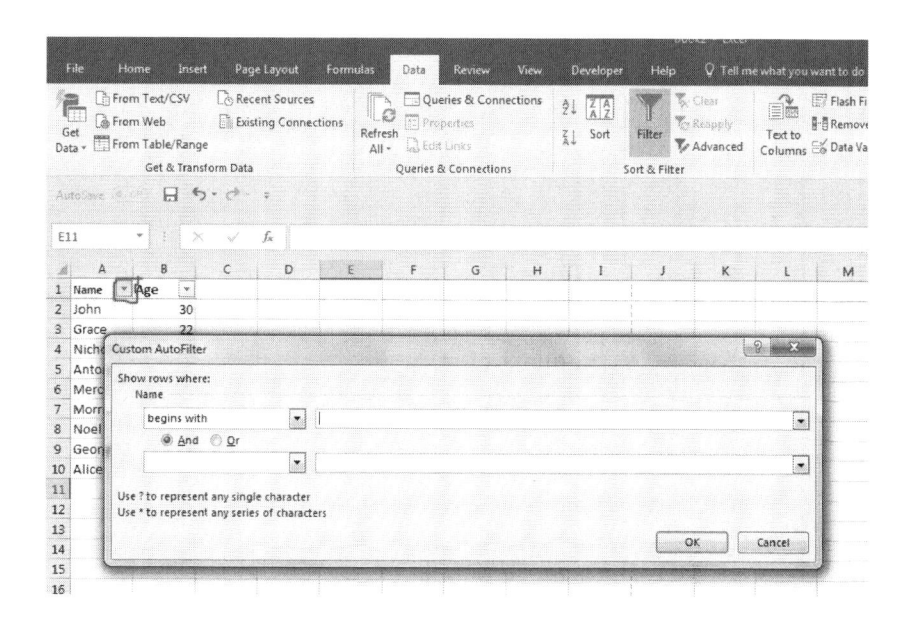

To see the names of individuals beginning with N, type "N" in the text field to the right of "begins with".

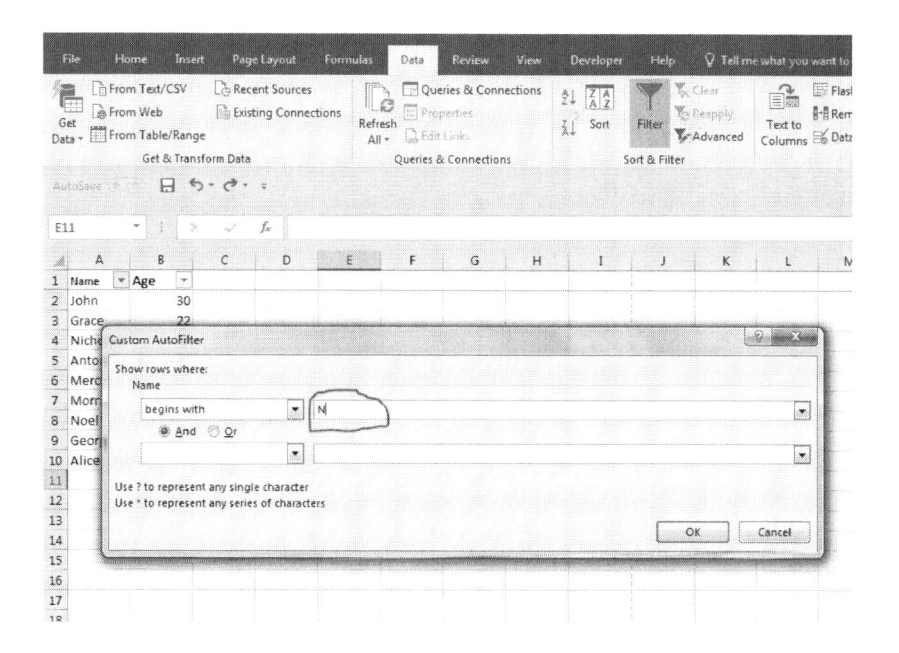

You can then Click OK button and see what happens. You will see that the results will filtered to get the names of the individuals beginning with "N" only. This is shown below:

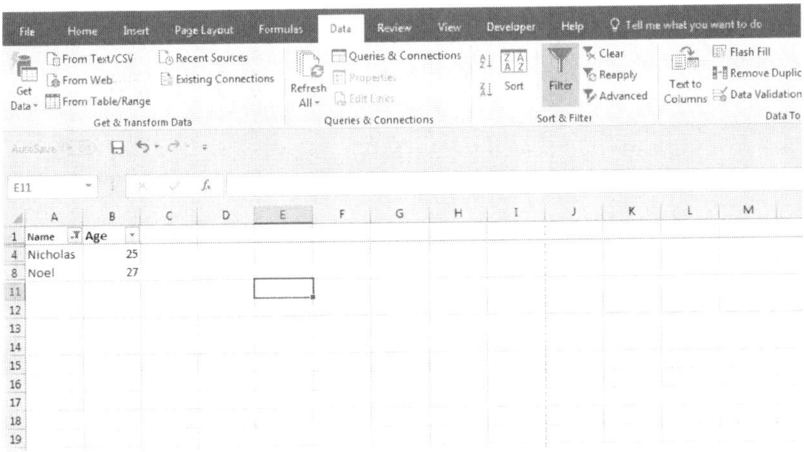

To filter the results by age, you have to click the drop down on the right of Age. You can then click the "Number Filters" option and choose the criteria to be used for filtering. If you need to see the names of individuals are less than 30, click "Less Than..." and you will get a dialog where you can specify the age value as shown below. Type 30 then click OK button:

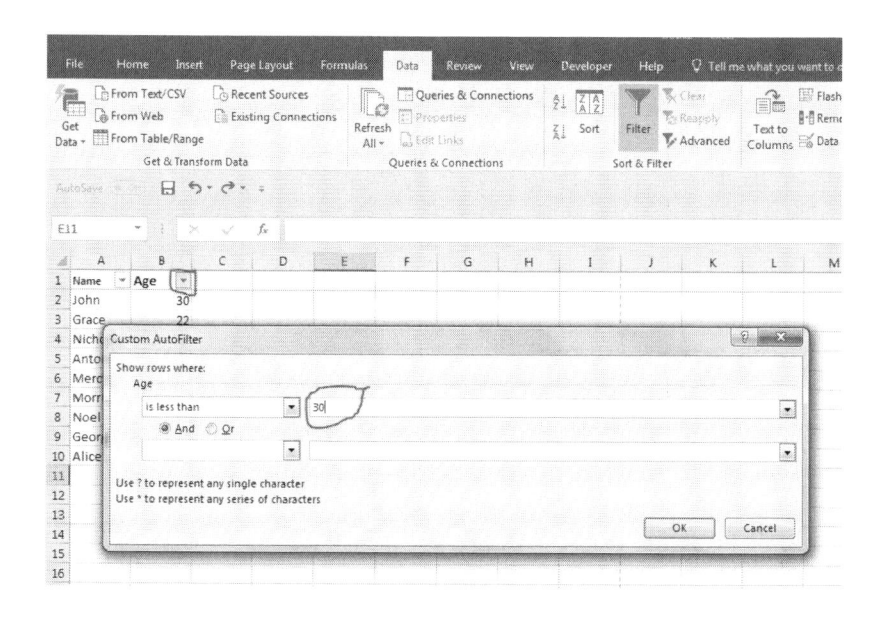

After clicking the OK button, the results will be filtered as shown below:

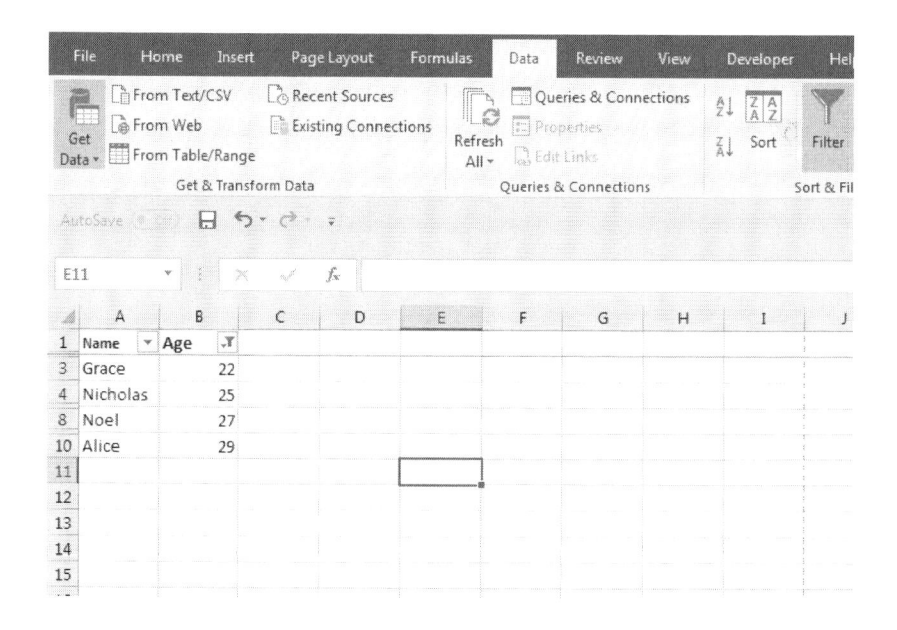

51

Only the names of individuals with an age less than 30 are shown.

Grouping and Ungrouping

With groups in Excel, it becomes easy for you to view and hide any unnecessary details from columns or rows. Groups can also be used for analyzing data that belongs to some common category.

Suppose we need to group the names in our sheet into males and females and get their average age. This can be done as follows:

Right click on Age; choose Insert, then "Entire column". Give the column the name Gender. You can then put female for the ladies and male for the males so that you end up with the following sheet:

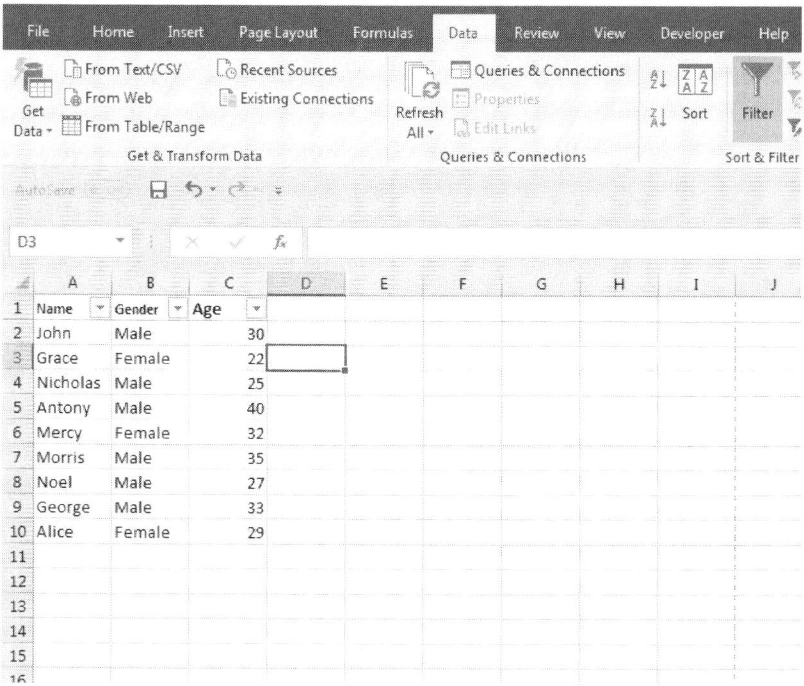
File
Home
Insert
Page Layout
Formulas
Data
Review
View
Developer
Help
Get Data
From Text/CSV
From Web
From Table/Range
Recent Sources
Existing Connections
Get & Transform Data
Refresh All
Queries & Connections
Properties
Edit Links
Queries & Connections
Sort
Filter
Sort & Filter
D3
Name
Gender
Age
John
Male
30
Grace
Female
22
Nicholas
Male
25
Antony
Male
40
Mercy
Female
32
Morris
Male
35
Noel
Male
27
George
Male
33
Alice
Female
29

We now need to group the males and the females separately then get their average age. Do this. Select all the rows and columns with data. Click the Data tab, and then click the "Group" drop-down, then select "Group..." You will get a new dialog as shown below:

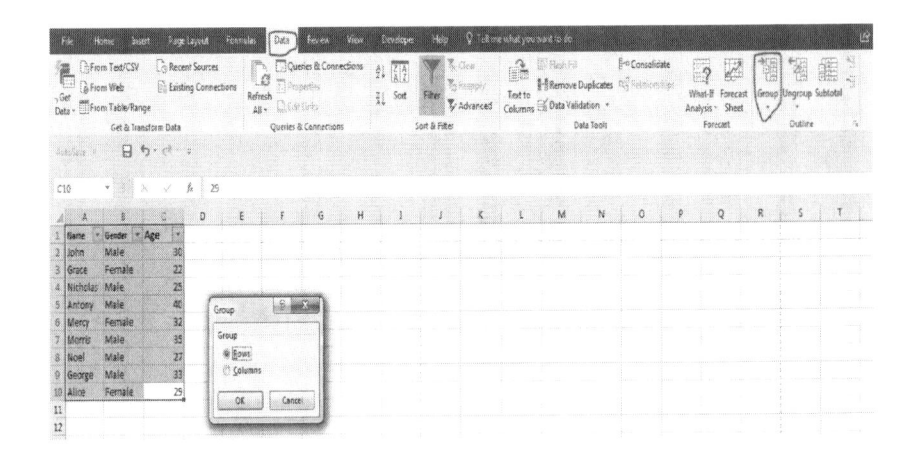

Ensure that you have the option for Rows selected, and then click the OK button. The males and the females will then be grouped into their own categories. We now need to get the average for each of these.

Begin by selecting the whole data. Click the Data tab then click the Subtotal dropdown button. You will get a pop up window. For "At each Change in:", put Gender, for "Use function", select "Average" and for "Add subtotal to:" set to "Score". You should now have the following window:

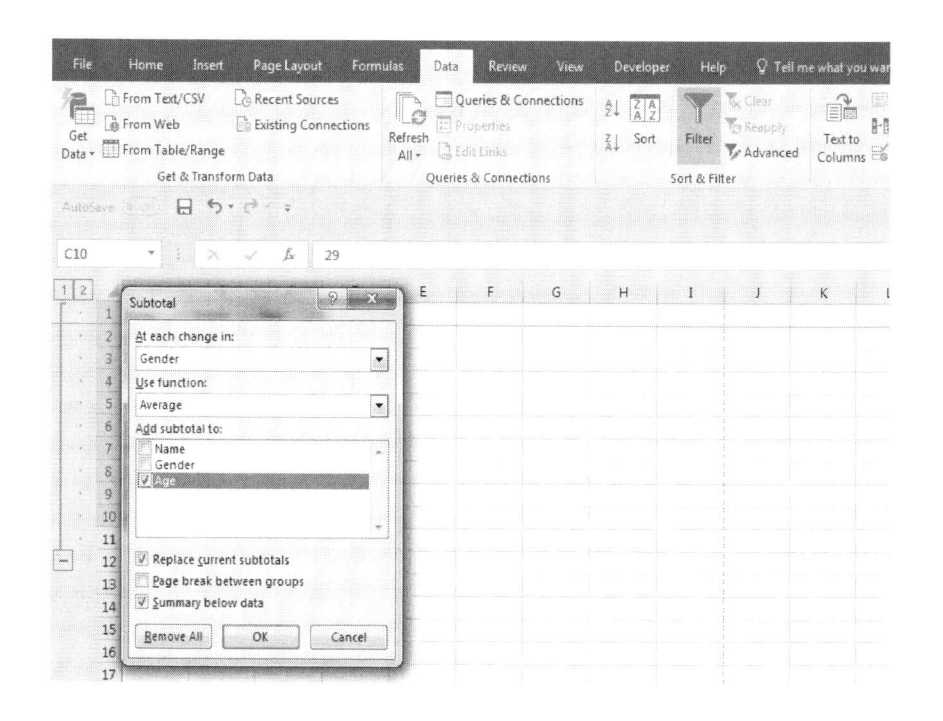

You can then click the "OK" button and you will be given the average for the data.

Chapter 6- Data Sorting

Sorting in Excel means arranging the rows based on column contents. A good example of such an application is when you need to sort the names in your sheet in an alphabetical order. You may also be in need of sorting out your data from the smallest to the largest or the largest to the smallest.

Suppose we need to sort the data based on column "Gender". We can do it as follows.

Select the column by which you need to sort the data; in this case, it's Gender. Click the DATA tab, and then click the Sort button. A dialog will appear. To sort the data based on the column that you have just selected, click the radio button for the second option, that is, **Continue with the selection,** but if you need to sort based on the other columns, click the first option, that is, **Expand Selection**. You can then click the "Sort":

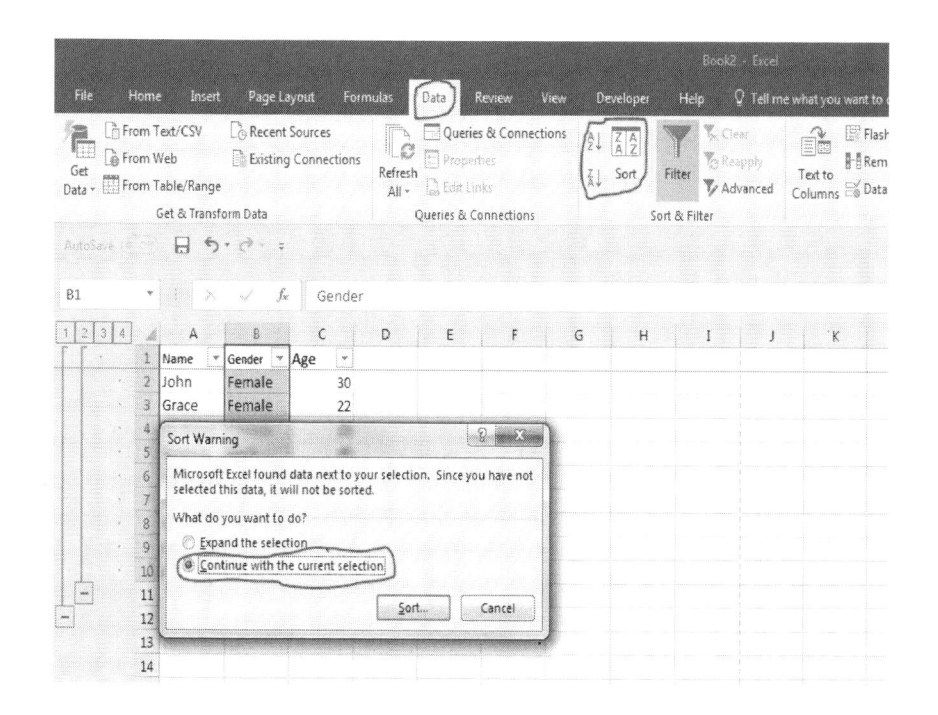

You will notice that the data will be sorted.

Chapter 7- Ranges

A cell is simply a single element in Excel capable of holing a value, text or even a formula. Each cell in Excel is denoted by an address that includes both the row and column number. We start with the letter denoting the column then the number denoting the row the cell is at. A cell C2 is at column C and row 2.

A range is simply a group of cells. To designate an address for a range, you use the address of the cell at the top-left and the address of the cell at bottom-right. These two are separated using a colon. Example A2:B2.

There are various ways through which you can select a range. With the mouse, you can simply press and hold down the left button then drag as you highlight the cells for the range. If you reach the end of the screen, you will notice that your worksheet ill roll. You can also use the keyboard to select a range. Just click the cell where the range begins, hold down the shift key then use the arrow keys to highlight the cells for the rage. You can press the F8 key on the keyboard, and then use the navigation keys to move the cell pointer in order to highlight the range. When you need to return the navigation keys to a normal movement, you will have to again press the F8 key.

You can also type a range address or cell address then hit the enter key. The specified range will then be selected.

Chapter 8- Formulas

Formulas make it easy for you to work with spreadsheets in Excel. With formulas, you can perform various calculations on the data in your Excel sheets. Formulas perform some calculations on your data then they return a result. The formulas use a number of operators and functions in order to perform calculations on both numbers and text. The numbers and text to be worked on by the formulas and functions can be found in other cells of the spreadsheet.

Creating Formulas

To create a formula in Excel, we type it in the formula bar. The excel formulas begin with an equal (=) sign. To specify the cells the formula should get the data from, you can type the cells manually, or you can point the formula to the cells. The pointing method is easy and more powerful compared to the typing method. If you want to use an in-built function, you can click the cell or just drag through the range of cells that you need for definition of the function arguments. This should be done in the Arguments dialog box for Functions.

Once you have completely typed in a formula, Excel gives you the result immediately. Example, in the following sheet:

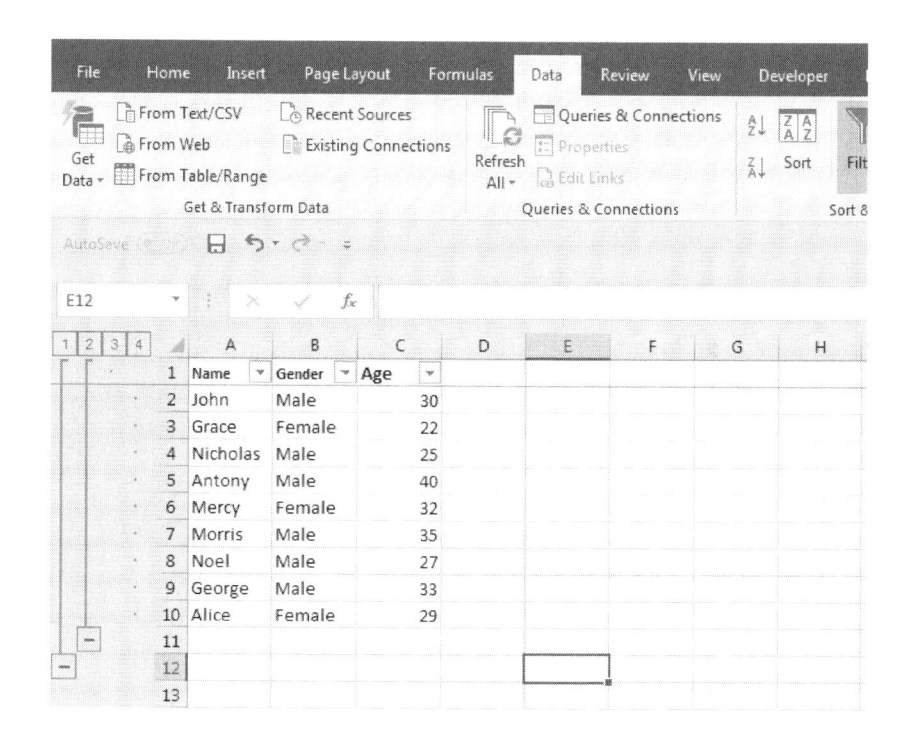

	A	B	C
1	Name	Gender	Age
2	John	Male	30
3	Grace	Female	22
4	Nicholas	Male	25
5	Antony	Male	40
6	Mercy	Female	32
7	Morris	Male	35
8	Noel	Male	27
9	George	Male	33
10	Alice	Female	29

We can compare the values of cells C2 and cell C6 to determine if they are the same in terms of value. This can be done by first clicking o an empty cell within the Excel sheet, then typing the following formula in the formula bar:

=C2=C6

This is shown below:

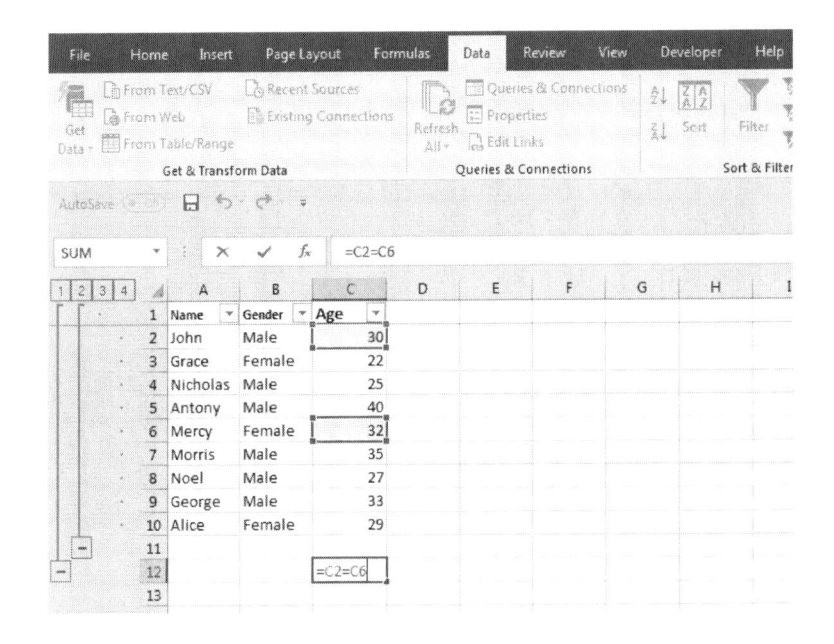

I had first clicked on cell C12. As I type the formula on the formula bar, it is also shown in that cell. Once I press the enter key, I get the following result:

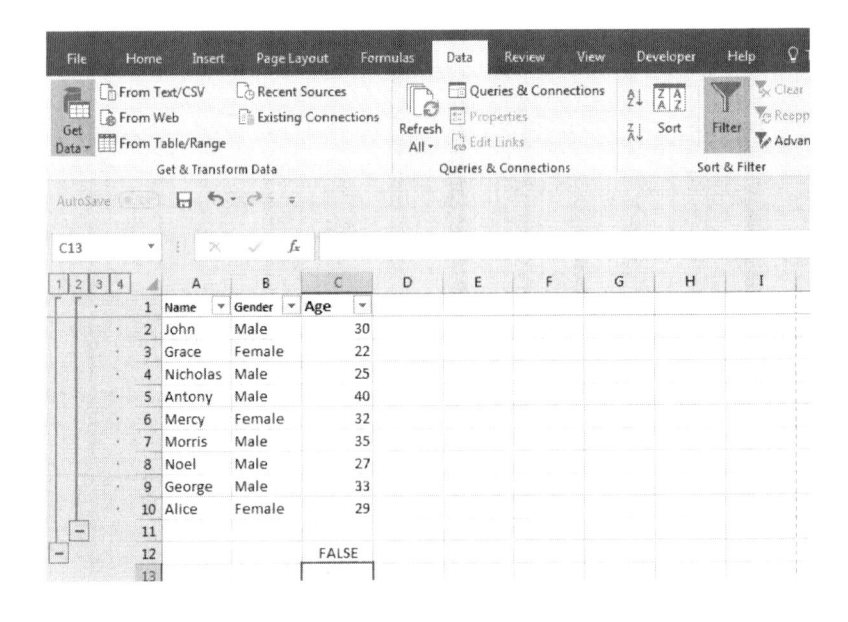

62

The result is FALSE, which means that the values of the two cells are not equal. If we compared two cells with equal values, then the result should be true.

Copying Formulas

Copying formulas is a very common task when using Excel sheets. When a formula is using cell reference rather than constant values, it becomes easy to copy a formula from one place to another place that needs the same formula. Excel makes the task easy as it automatically adjusts the cell references to match the cells that you need to refer to after making a copy of a formula. This is done through a feature called *relative cell addresses*. With this mechanism, the column references in a cell address in a formula change to their new column position while the row references change to fit their current row position. Suppose we have a spreadsheet with the following data:

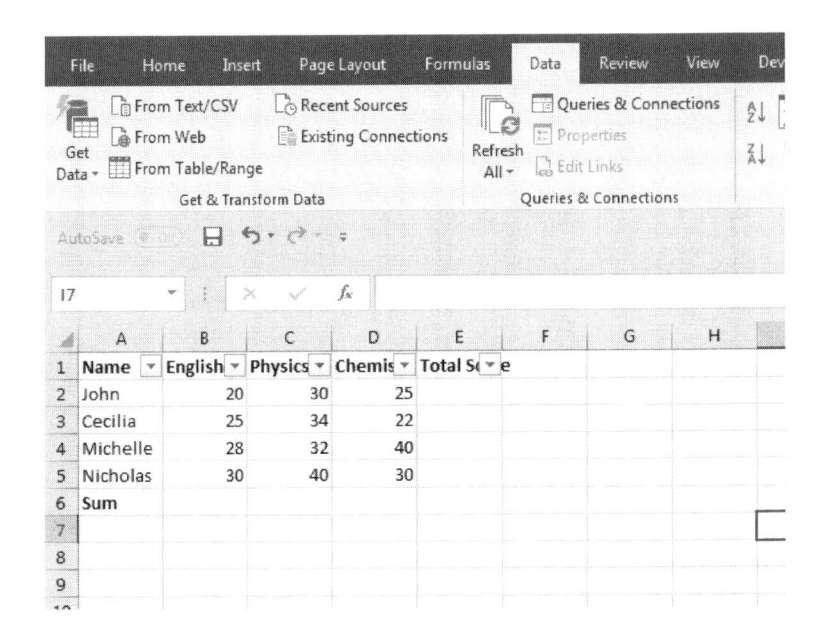

We need to begin by calculating the sum for each row. We begin by writing the formula for calculating this sum for column 2, that is, cell B2 to cell B5. This is shown below:

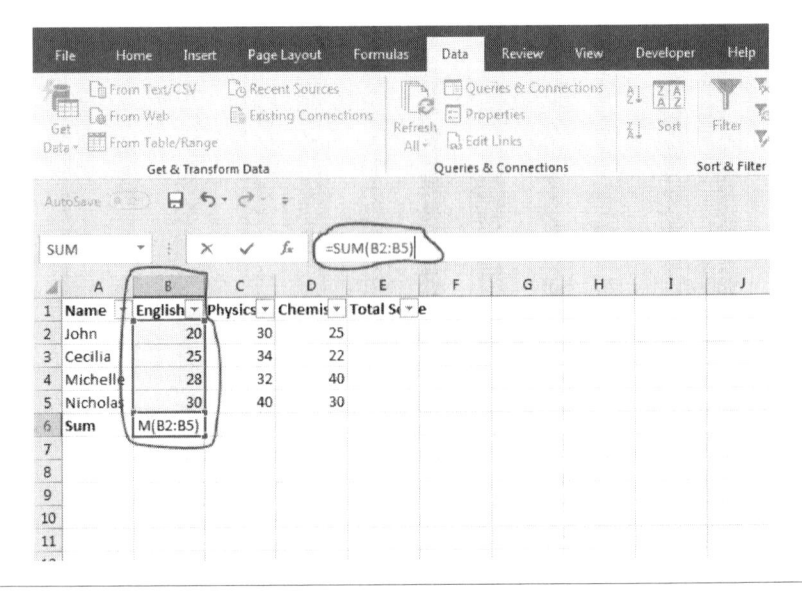

When I press the enter key, I will get the necessary result. Once we have written the formula in the 6th row, it is possible for us to drag it to the cells on the right and it will get copied. That is how Excel makes the work easy for us.

Cell References

Majority of the formulas that are written include references to rages or cells. Such references enable the formulas to dynamically work with data that is in the ranges or cells. A good example is when your formula is referring to cell B2 and you need to change the value of the cell. The result of the formula should automatically reflect the change in the value of the cell. If you had not used references when creating or writing the formula, then you will have to change the formula so that you may see at the same time see the change.

When using a range or cell reference in a formula, there are three types of references that you can use namely absolute, relative and mixed references.

Relative Cell References

The column and row references may change after copying the formula to another cell as the references are offsets from current row and column. The default setting is that Excel creates relative cell references in the formulas. The previous example demonstrates how relative cell references are used in Excel, so no need of doing it again.

Absolute Cell References

The column and row references don't change after copying the formula since the reference denotes an actual cell address. The absolute cell reference makes use of two dollar signs ($) in the address. One signs if for the row number and the other for the column letter. Example, B2.

The following shows how we can use absolute reference in a formula:

=SUM ($B2:B5)

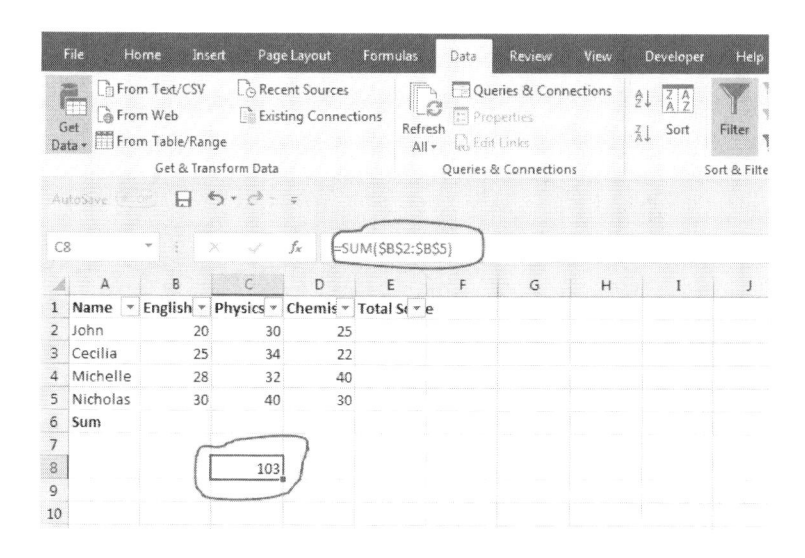

When I press the enter key, I get the sum of the range of cells specified in the formula. That is how absolute cell referencing works in Excel formulas.

Mixed Cell References

In this case, only one part of the address is made to be absolute. Example, $B2 or B$2. Consider the practical example given below:

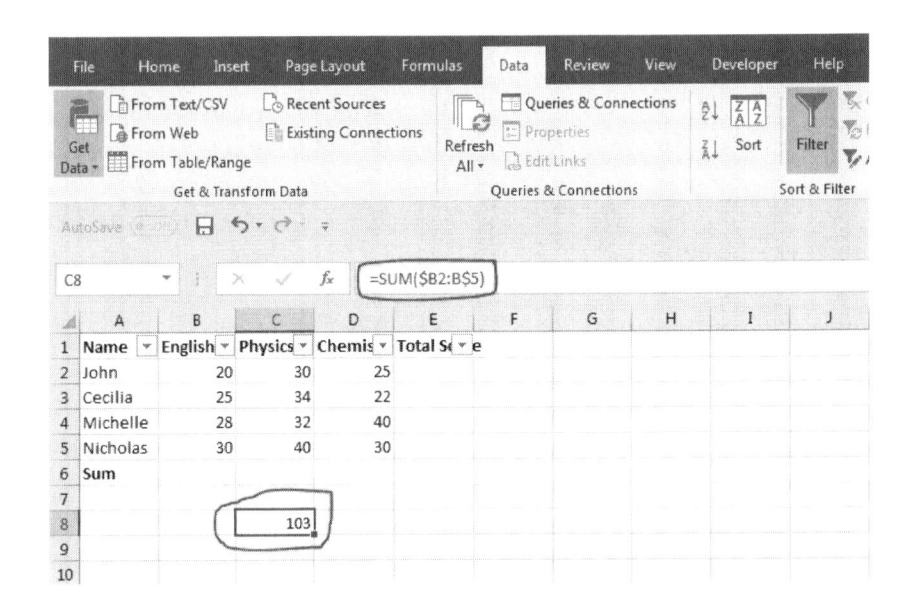

Functions in Formulas

With functions, you can have very powerful working formulas in Excel. Most formulas use the worksheet functions that are already available. With functions, you can carry out complex tasks that can be hard when one is using only operators. Examples of functions are the SIN and LOG functions that can help in calculation of Sin or Log rations. With operators alone, it is hard for you to calculate such ratios.

After typing the equal sign, then followed by any letter of the alphabet, you will be presented with a list of functions that begin with that letter. You can then choose the function that you need from this list.

Example: Suppose you have a range of cells with numeric values and you need to find the minimum of these. It will be hard for you to get the answer with a basic formula. However, this is possible with a function known as MIN. We need to get the minimum value with the range of cell B2 to cell B5. We can use the formula =MIN (B2:B5) as shown below:

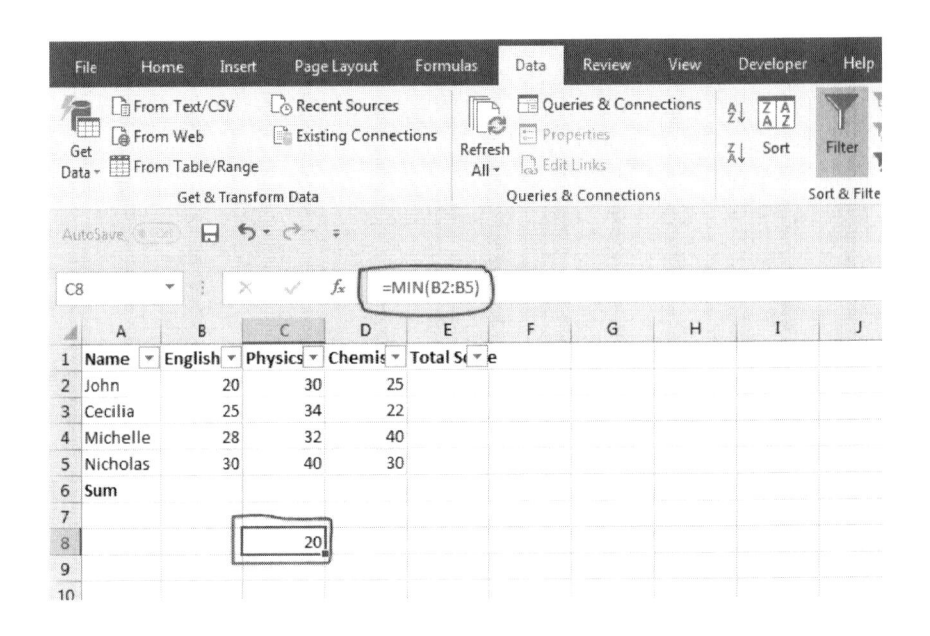

	A	B	C	D	E
1	Name	English	Physics	Chemis	Total S
2	John	20	30	25	
3	Cecilia	25	34	22	
4	Michelle	28	32	40	
5	Nicholas	30	40	30	
6	Sum				
7					
8			20		

C8: =MIN(B2:B5)

Sometimes, you may need to find the value contained in a particular cell then take an action based on this. This can only be done with functions. For example, if the above case, we may need to determine whether John scored 25 and above or below in English and give the necessary comment about the score, maybe good, bad, fair etc. In such a case, we can use an IF function. Don't be shocked, Excel supports like programming like constructs. Example:

=IF (B2>25,"Good","Fair")

This formula can be used as shown in the screenshot given below:

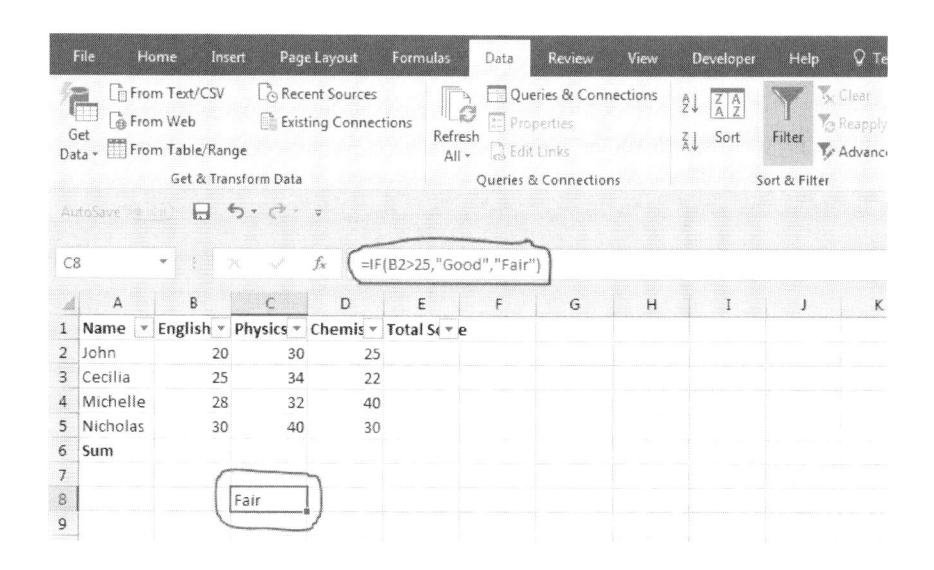

The condition has been specified, and then we have specified the outputs, each within double quotes. The result to be shown if the condition is true is written first, which in our case is "Good". The result to be shown if the condition is false is written second, which in our case is "Fair".

To get the average score in a subject like English, we can use the formula given below:

=AVERAGE (B2:B5)

This is shown in the screenshot given below:

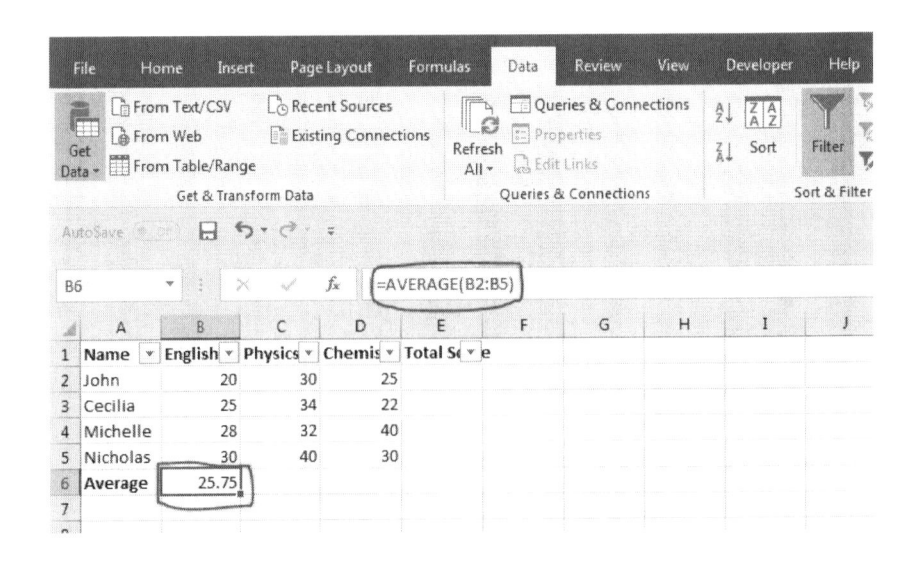

To get the maximum value within a range of cells, we use the MAX function. To get the highest score in English, we can use the following function:

=MAX (B2:B5)

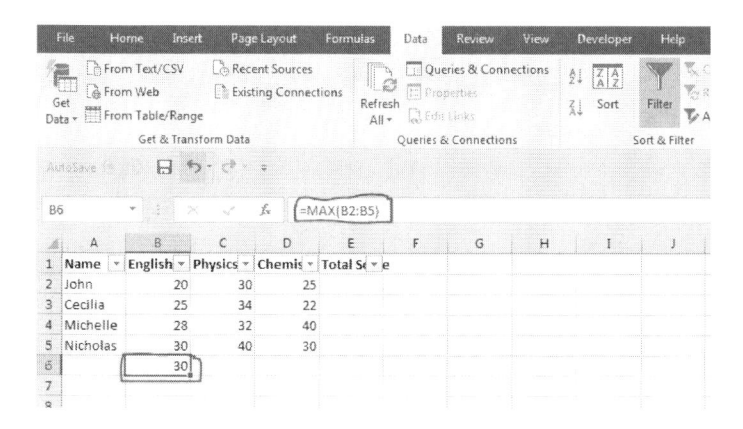

This shows the highest score in English was 30. In the above case, we can use the LEN function for *length* to determine the number of characters in the name *Michelle*. This is shown below:

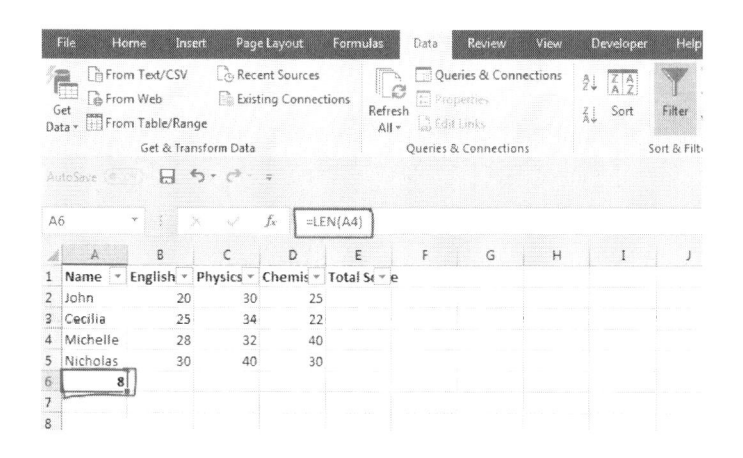

The output shows that the name has 8 characters.

Excel also has functions that can be used to operate on strings rather than numbers. Suppose we need to print the first 3 characters of the string in cell A2, we can run the LEFT function as shown below:

=LEFT (A2,3)

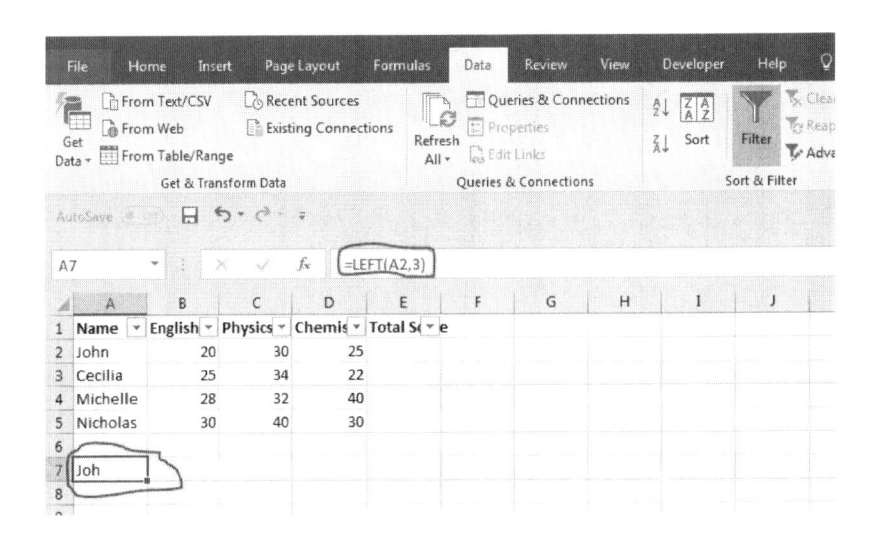

As you can see above, the output is Joh. The cell A2 has the name *John*. Excel begins to count from the left until the third character, hence the source of the above output. It is not a must for us to reference a cell and print some text in the cell. We can pass some string to the LEFT function as shown below:

LEFT ("Excel",3)

In the above example, we are printing the first three characters in the *Excel* string. This is shown below:

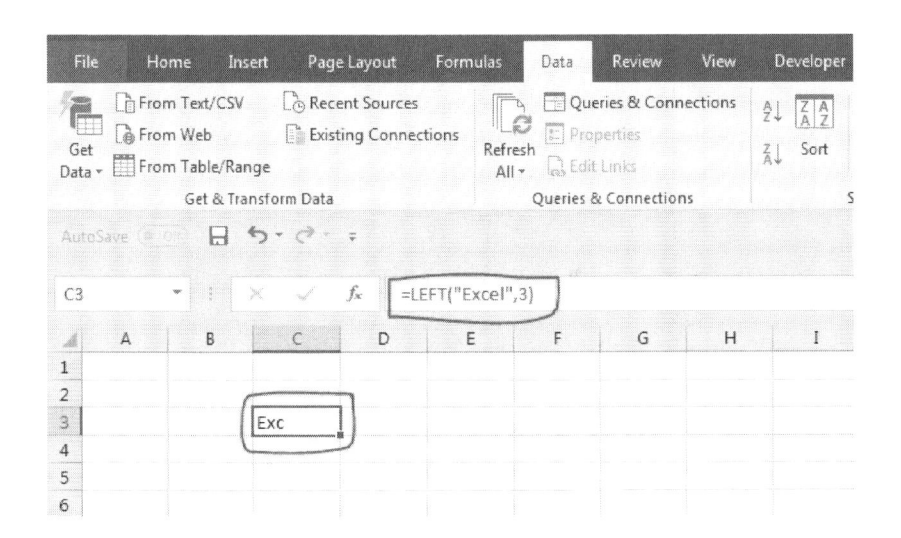

The LEFT function begins to count from the left-most character. With the RIGHT function, this is opposite as it begins to count from the right-most character. Again, you can a string directly to the function or even a cell with some text. Example:

=Right (A2,3)

We begin to count the text on cell A2 and display its last three characters. This is demonstrated below:

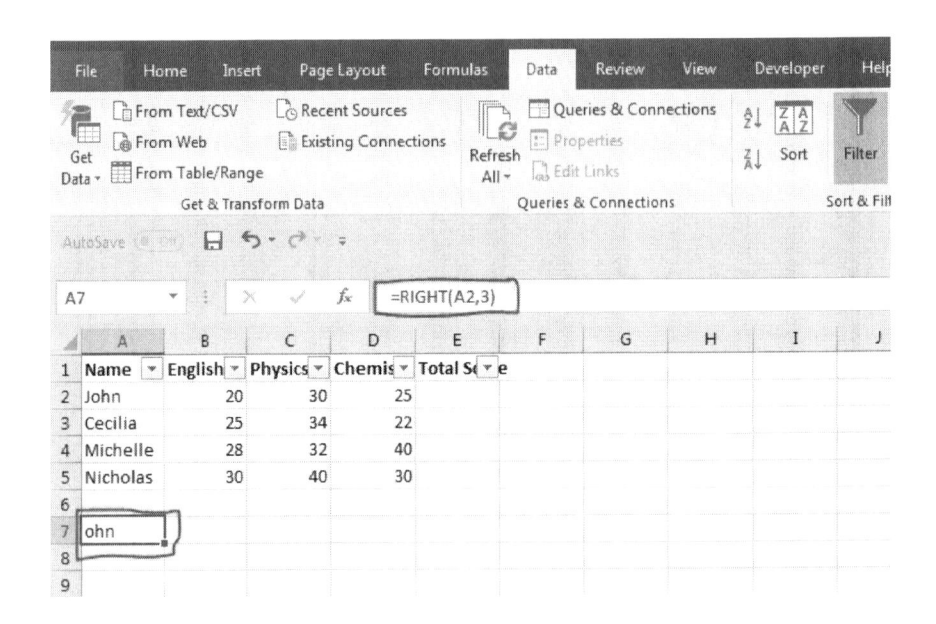

With a real text, this function also works excellently as shown below:

=RIGHT ("JOHN",3)

This is demonstrated below:

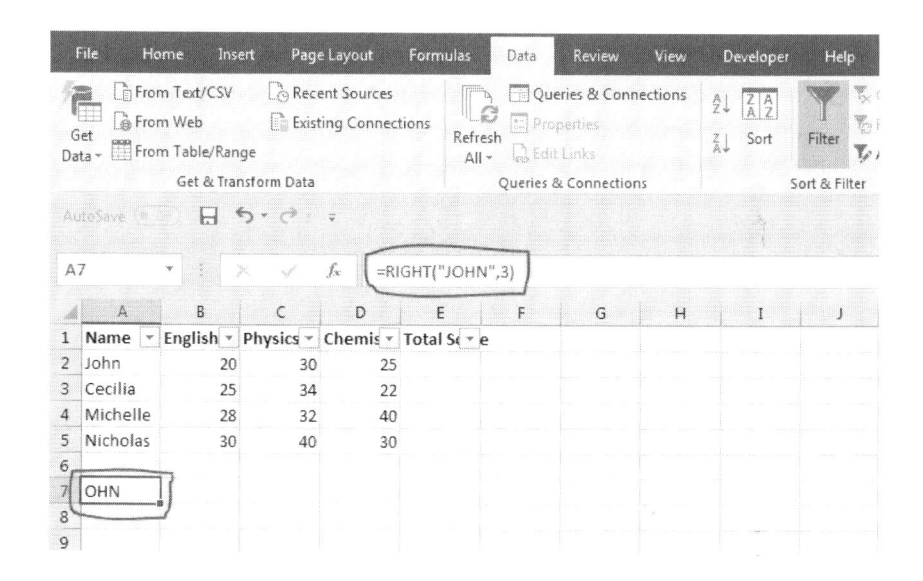

To begin counting from the middle of a string, we use the MID function. This begins counting from a specified position and counts until it reaches a specified position. Example:

=MID ("Physics",2,4)

This results into the result given below:

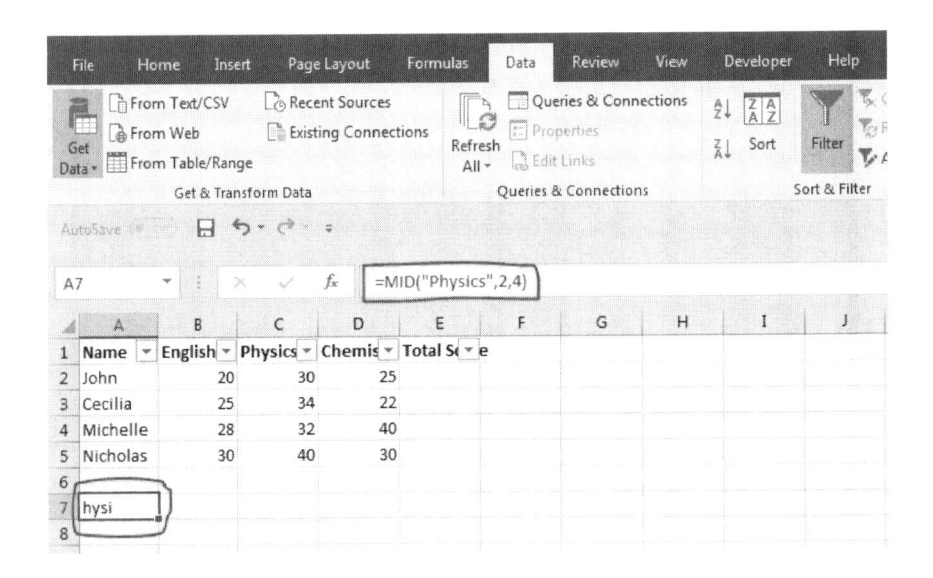

	A	B	C	D	E
1	Name	English	Physics	Chemis	Total S
2	John	20	30	25	
3	Cecilia	25	34	22	
4	Michelle	28	32	40	
5	Nicholas	30	40	30	
6					
7	hysi				
8					

Formula bar: =MID("Physics",2,4)

You can also pass a cell number to the function and it will count the cell's text as you have specified. To determine whether a string is text or not, use the ISTEXT function as shown below:

=ISTEXT ("Physics")

The result from the above function is TRUE since the argument passed to the function is a text, otherwise, the result would have been a FALSE.

With the FIND function, you can get the position at which the argument specified begins in the string. Note that this function is case sensitive. It can be used a shown below:

=FIND ("it","Arithmetic",1)

The result of the above function will be 3. This is because the "it" begins at position 3 in the string.

Excel also has the REPLACE function with which one can replace a string of text. You must specify the position from which the replacement should be done, the extent to which it will be done as well as the string to be used for replacement. Example:

=REPLACE ("Coming",4,3,"e")

In the above function, we are replacing the 3 characters from the fourth position. This means that the "ing" will be replaced with "e". This works as shown in the screenshot given below:

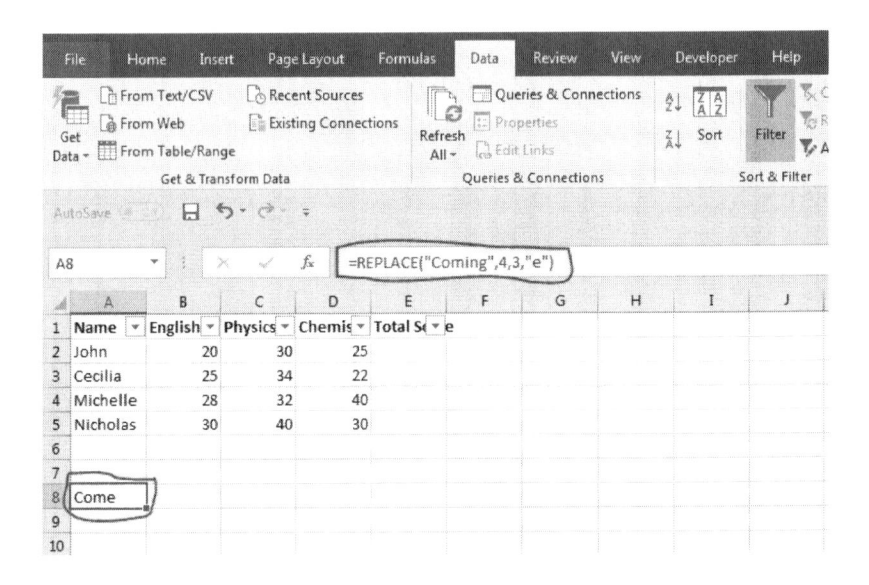

As shown above, the text "coming" has been modified to become "come".

Chapter 9- Working with Graphics

In Excel, various types of graphics are supported such as SmartArt, Shapes gallery, WordArt, Text Box etc. These can all be found under the Insert tab.

To insert a shape into your Excel Sheet, click the Insert tab. Next, click the "Shapes" dropdown then select the shape that you need to insert then click it.

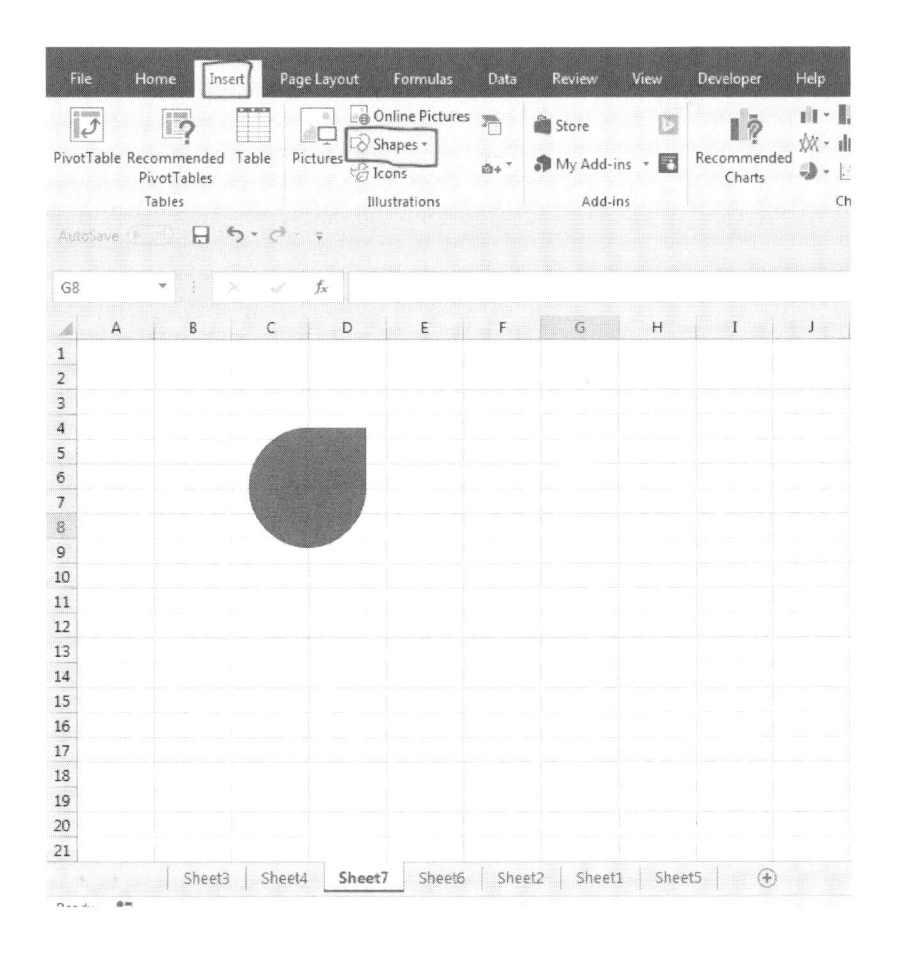

After clicking the shape, click the position in which you need it inserted and the shape will be inserted. You may need to recreate the shape that has been inserted. To do this, you only have to drag it using your mouse cursor.

You can also insert a SmartArt through the similar steps. To do this following the steps given below:

Click the Insert tab, and then click the SmartArt icon. After that, SmartArt dialogue will be opened as shown below:

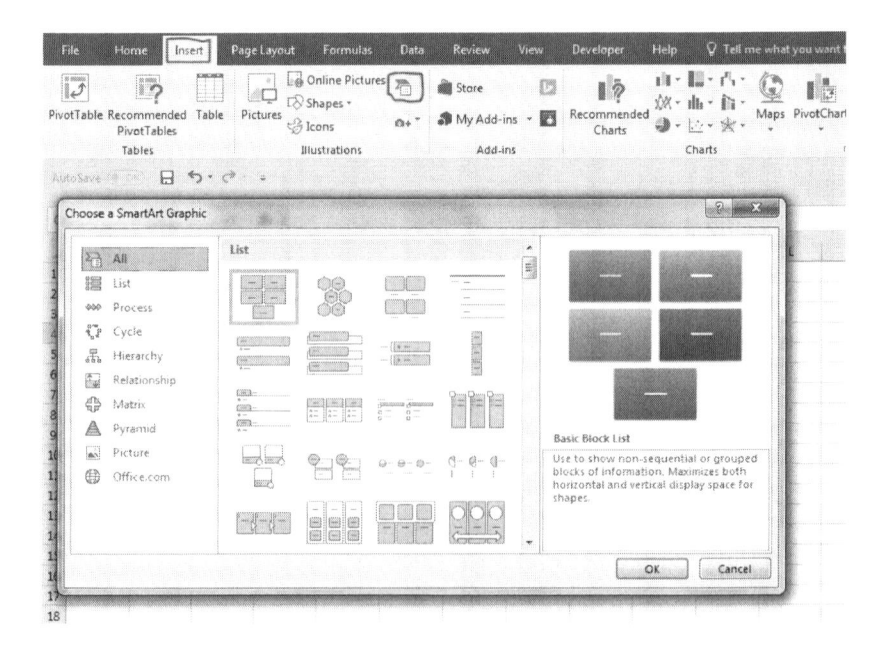

You can then choose the SmartArt that you need from the available ones. Identify the SmartArt that you need to insert then click it. Next, click the OK button for the SmartArt to be inserted. You can then edit the SmartArt to meet your requirements.

Chapter 10- Excel Macros

With Excel Macros, it is possible for you to automate nearly everything that you do with Excel. You can use the macro recorder to record tasks performed routinely, the procedure can be speeded up greatly and ensure that your tasks are performed in the same way every time you perform them.

To view the macros, click the View tab, then choose the "Macros" dropdown. You can then click "View Macros". Here is the dialog:

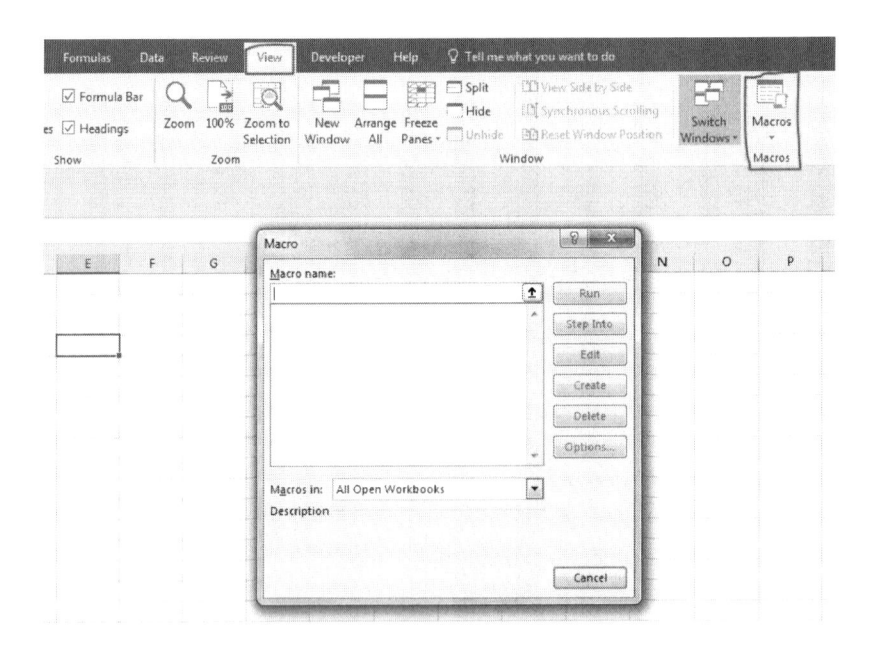

In the above dialog, you are allowed to choose a macro that you can edit or run.

You can also record a macro. This involves defining the settings for the new macro and starting the macro recorder. To do this, you only have clicked the macro recorder option from the Macros drop down. This gives you the dialog given below:

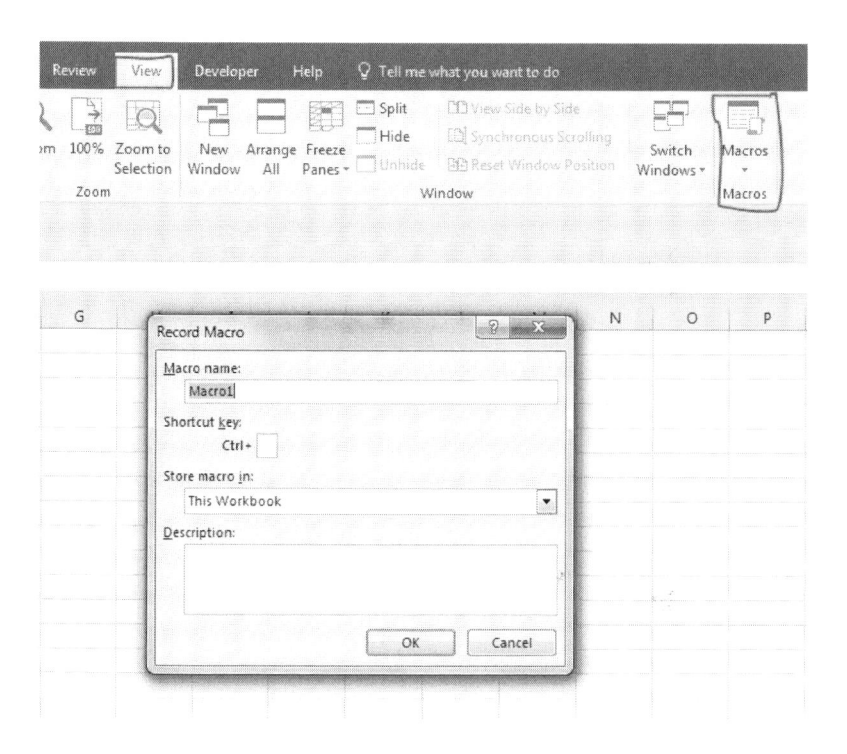

There are two ways through which you can create macros in Excel. You can use the macro recorder to record actions while undertaking them in the Excel worksheet. You can also open the Visual Basic Editor to enter the instructions that you need in the form of VBA code. We can demonstrate by creating a simple macro.

Click the View tab, head over to the Macros drop down then choose "Record Macro…" Give the Macro a name, choose where to store it then give it a description if possible. Next, click the OK button and recording of the macro will commence.

You can then do all the actions that you need to do repeatedly and the macro will record them. Once you are done with the recording process, feel free to stop the recording. To stop this, you only have to click the "Macros" drop down then choose "Stop Recording".

It is easy for you to edit the macro any time that you need. The process of editing the macro will simply take you to VBA programming editor. To edit a macro, you will have to click the View tab, open the Macros drop down then choose the 'View Macros" option. The dialog will appear and you will be able to see all the available macros.

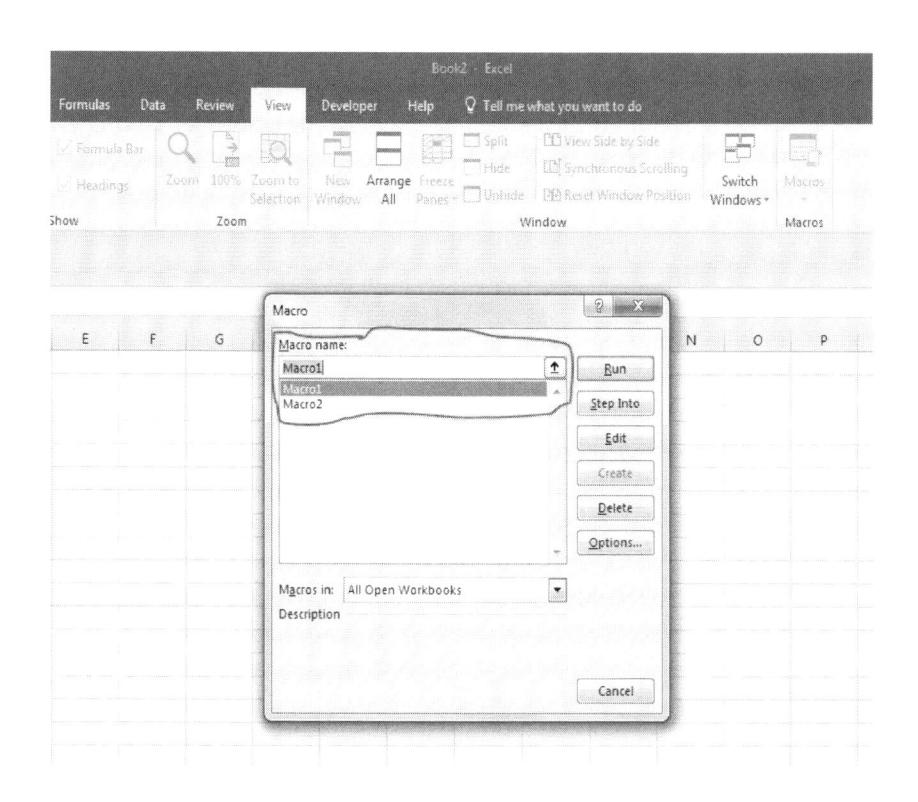

Select the Macro that you need to edit, and then click the Edit button located on the right side of the dialog. You will be taken to the VBA programming editor.

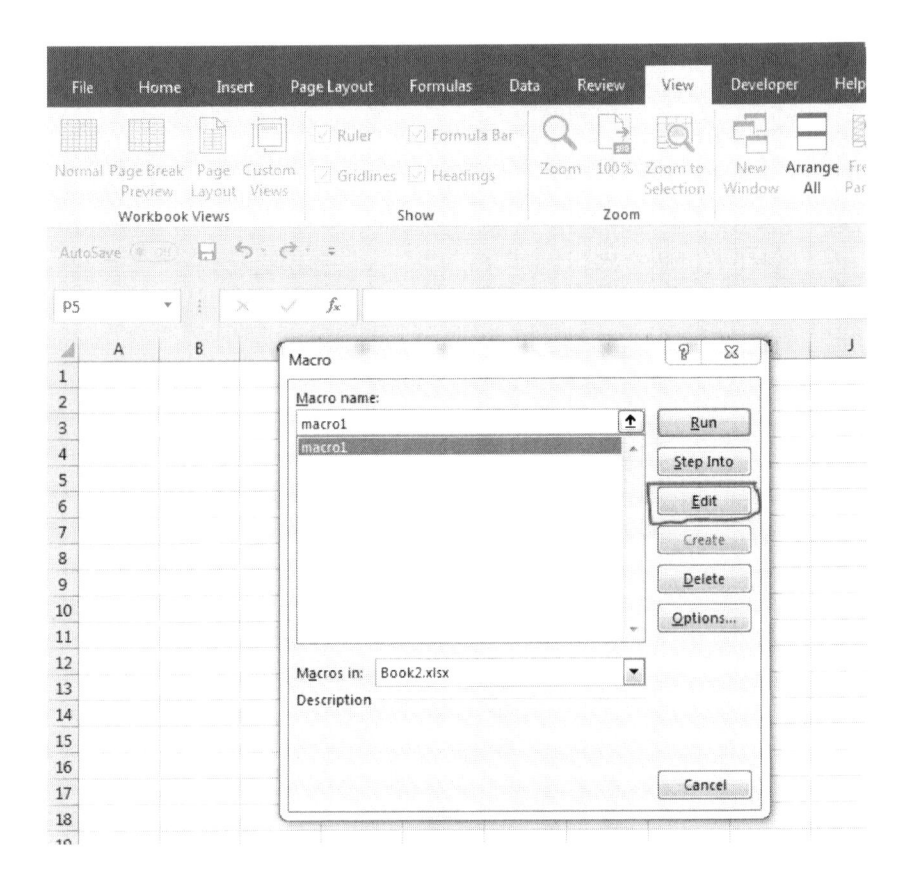

For you to edit the macro, you need some knowledge about VBA programming. This is the only way you can edit the macro. VBA is easy to learn, so you can start today.

Select the macro that you need to edit, and then click the "Edit" button located on the right side of the window. You will be taken to the VBA programming editor from which you will be able to edit the macro in the way that you want.

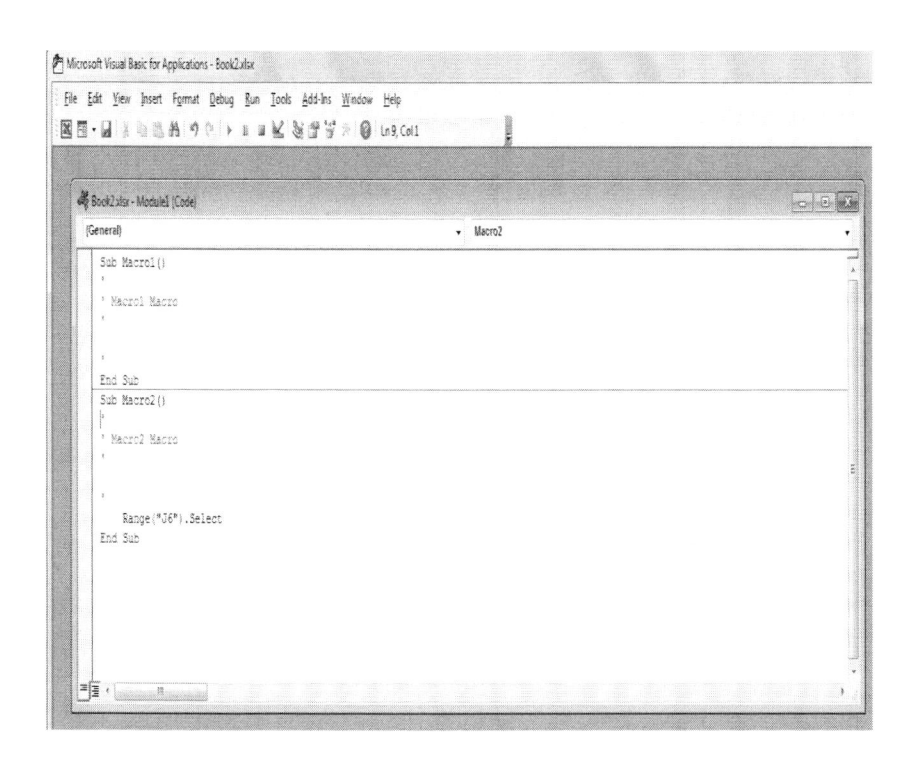

```
Sub Macro1()
'
' Macro1 Macro
'

'
End Sub
Sub Macro2()

' Macro2 Macro
'

'
    Range("J6").Select
End Sub
```

Chapter 11- Charts and Tables

Charts

Images, graphics and charts are good way to create a visual representation of data. Excel is capable of creating charts automatically for us. Excel provides us with the tools that we can use to create charts for our numeric data. This helps us get a way of representing data in the form of a summary.

There are various types of charts that are provided in Excel. To see them, follow the steps given below:

Begin by selecting some cells with numeric data on your spreadsheet. Next, click the Insert tab, then choose the "See All Charts" icon. A new pop up window will be shown. Just click the tab for "All Charts".

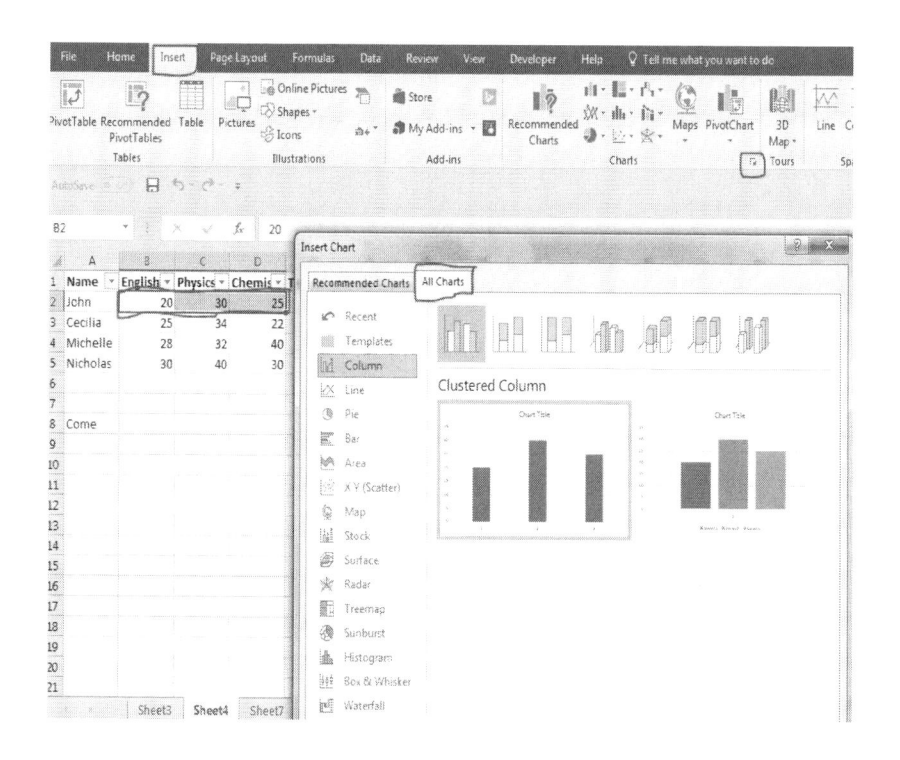

All the charts will be shown. To see how each of the charts appears like, you only have to click them from the list on the left of the pop up window. A column chart is good for showing a comparison of items. With a bar chart, you can get a comparison between individual items. With a pie chart, you can see and compare the size of an item relative to the other items in the same series. With a line chart, you can see how data varies during a particular period of time.

To create a chart, you should begin by selecting the cells with the data for which you need to create a chart. Next, you click the chart you need from the ones provided in the ribbon. These are shown below:

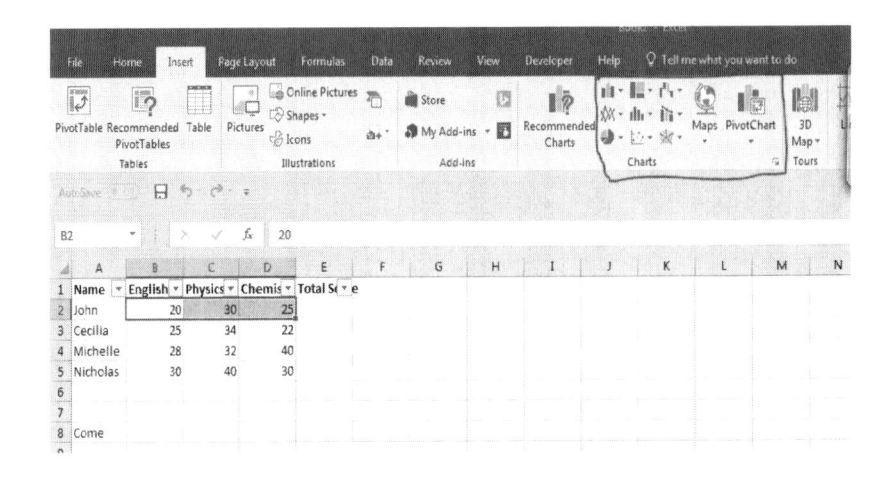

After clicking any of the above charts, it will be inserted into the sheet. However, you may not see the chart that you need in the ribbon. To see additional charts, just click the "See All Charts" icon which is shown below:

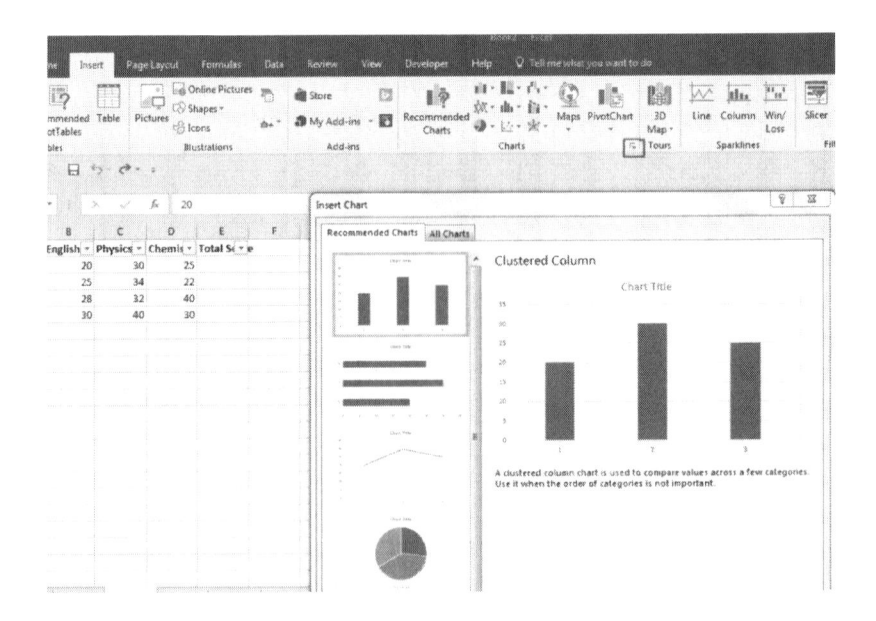

A popup shows with various charts that you can use for your data. You only have to identify the chart that you need, click it then click the OK button located at the bottom to insert it into your worksheet.

In my case, I have inserted a 2D pie-chart for the three cells with data. This is shown below:

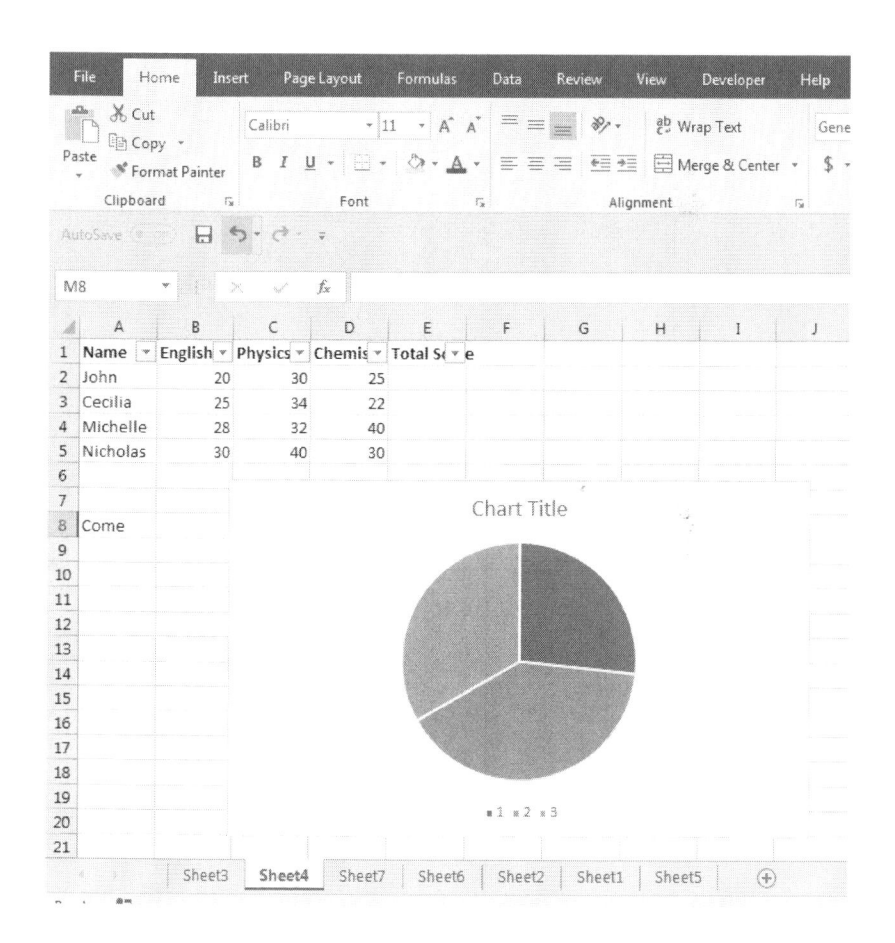

Notice that you are allowed to change the details of the chart like the title.

After inserting a chart into your data, you can edit it anytime that you need. To do this, just right click the chart, and then choose "Select Data..." A new window will popup and it will show the cells with the data that you have used to draw the current chart. This is shown below:

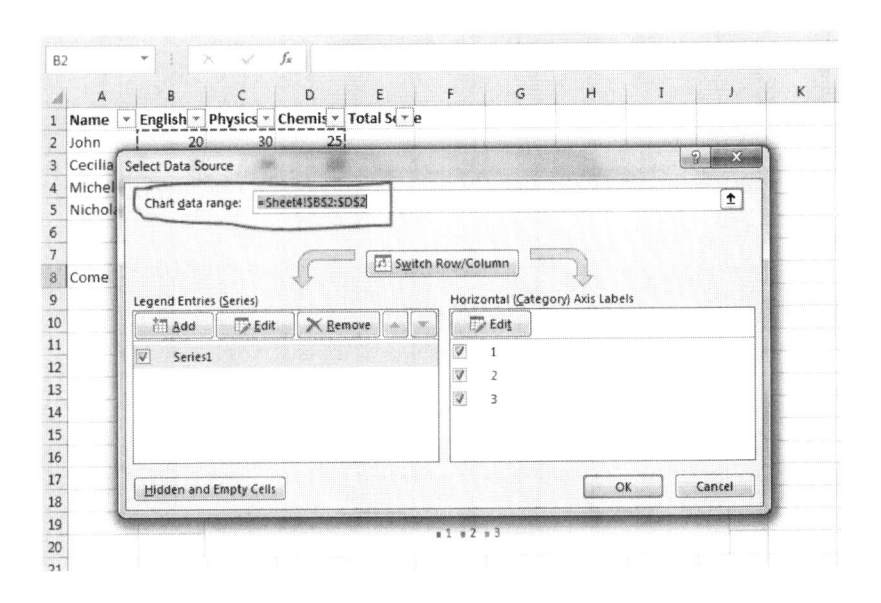

To generate a new chart, you only have to specify some new cells whose data you are to use. Like in my case, I can now choose to generate a pie chart for the data contained in cells B3 to cell D3. This is shown below:

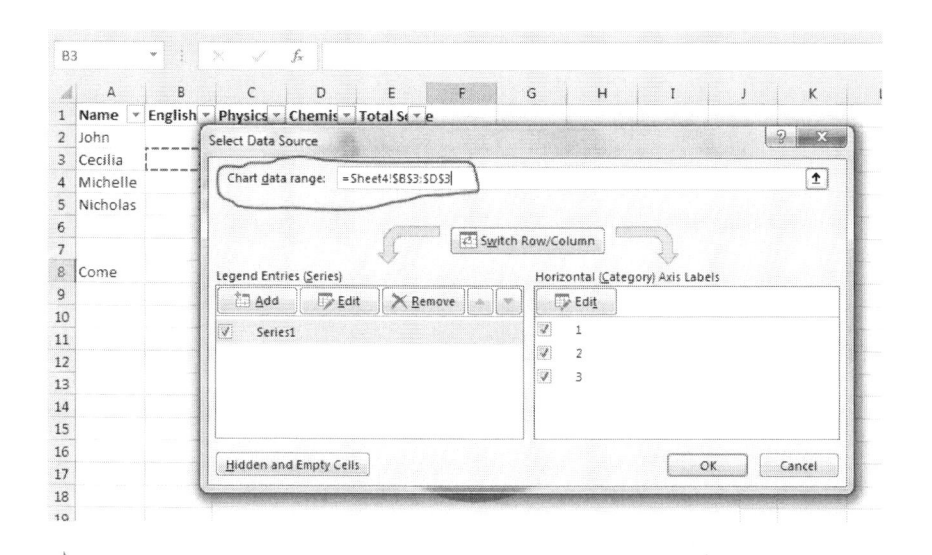

I have changed from cells B2-D2 to B3-D3. Note that the name of the sheet has not changed, but you can still change it if you need to use data from a different worksheet. Once done, click the OK button located at the bottom and a new chart will be generated. Note that the new data will be used for generating the chart. You will see that the chart will change since new data has been use for generating the chart.

To change the elements of the chart, maybe the title, label etc., first, click the chart to select it, click the + icon located to the right of the chart. To add any feature, activate its checkbox, to remove the feature, de-activate the checkbox.

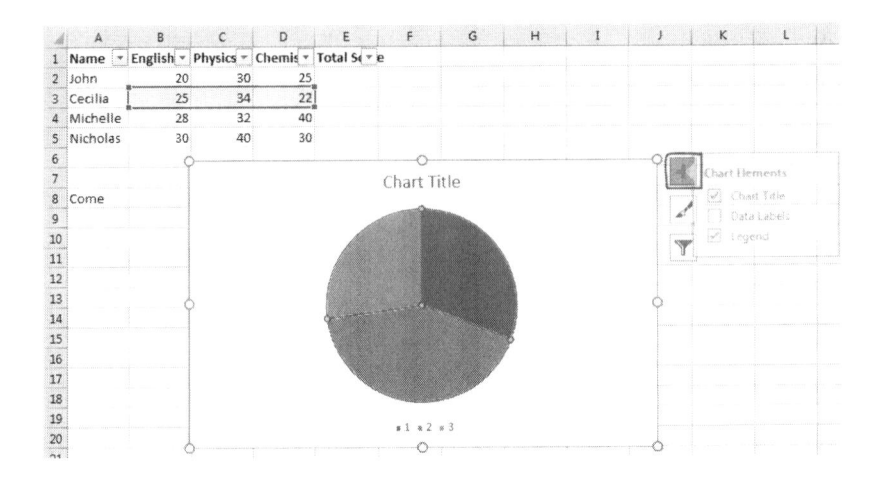

You can also change the style of the chart that you have inserted. If it is a pie chart, there are different styles of a pie chart that you can use. To see choose the style that you need, click the brush-like icon below the + icon. Note that you must first select the chart by clicking it.

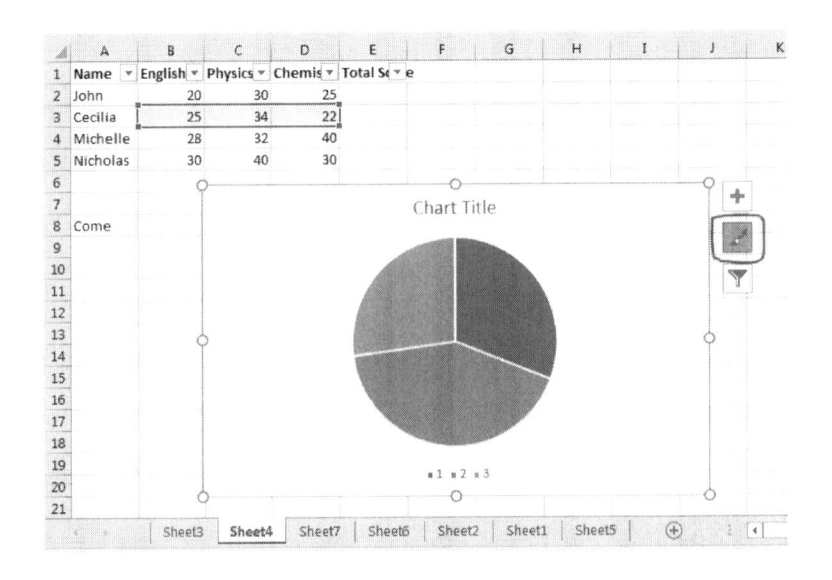

To select a style, just click it and you will see the chart change.

Data Tables

Sometimes, you may be in need of analyzing huge amounts of data and come up with reports. This can be done with data tables. A data table allows you to see different results by changing some input cell in the formula. You can access a data table by navigating through the Data tab, then clicking the "What-If Analysis" dropdown. You can then choose "Data Table" from the options that are provided. This is shown below:

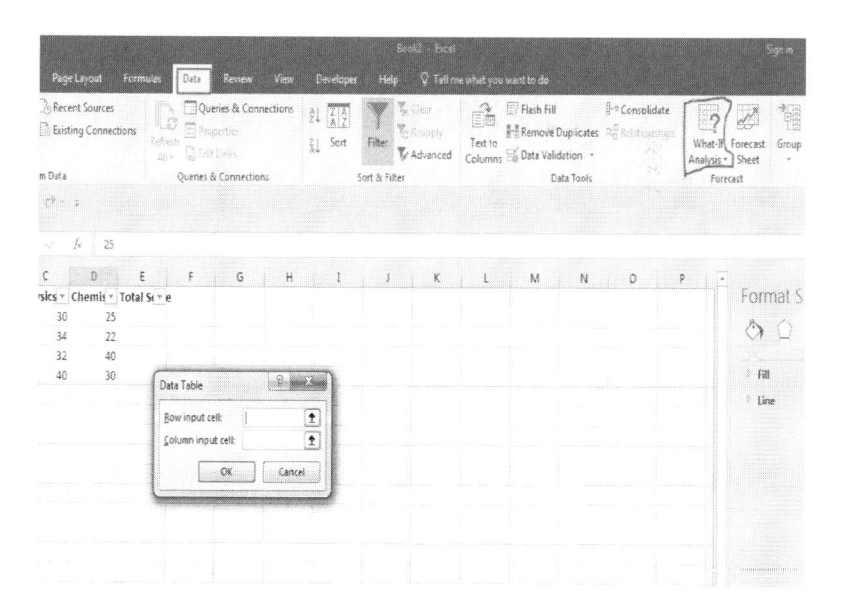

In the dialog box, you are asked to provide the *Row Input Cell* and the *Column Input Cell*. You can provide the values for these, which are cell addresses, then click the OK button. The data table will be generated for you. The formula for the table will also be generated.

Conclusion

This marks the end of this guide. Excel is a tool developed by Microsoft on which you can create a spreadsheet. You can add any type of data to the spreadsheet. Excel provides many tools that can be used for manipulation of the data you add to your spreadsheet. It has formulas and functions that you can use for performing various operations on the data. For instance, you can perform various arithmetic operations on the data using the regular arithmetic operators. Excel also has various functions that can be used to operate on the data. If the data is numerical, you can calculate several measures such as average etc. You can also compare different values in the data. Due to the ease of use Excel is highly used in many institutions and companies for data analysis.

Printed in Great Britain
by Amazon